THE CARING ECONOMY:

How to Win With Corporate Social Responsibility

First Edition

By Toby Usnik

Amazon Kindle Direct Publishing

New York, New York

For my mother, Sally

Contents

INTRODUCTION

> "Life is a journey, not a destination."
> – Ralph Waldo Emerson

Through my 30-year odyssey in the corporate world, I have not only witnessed but helped advance the evolution of Corporate Social Responsibility (CSR). I have been part of a sea-change of businesses stepping up to make a better world through their business practices. The early roots of CSR were more local, charitable, and almost quaint; however, today CSR is global, strategic, and business critical.

By the early 1990s an elite group of mostly multinationals such as GE, Tata, and American Express were leading the way with CSR and seen regularly in rankings such as Fortune magazine's 100 Best Companies to Work For. As we entered the new millennium, however, the list of companies and the areas of CSR blossomed beyond these brands and issues such as domestic partner benefits, family leave and gender equality – to name a few important causes – to include climate change, income disparity, consumer privacy, and more. Along the way, winning companies and employees were setting a new tone for business by anticipating their customers' evolving concerns.

Today's CSR practitioners are pioneering by setting a fresher, more aspirational tone for business and quickly following with inspirational and impactful action. They are expressing strong points of view and taking action in ways that once would have seemed too radical, idealistic, or impractical. Thirty years into my CSR journey, I see business winners advocating fiercely for compassion, inclusion, and transparency in their operations. They do this not just for commercial gain, but also to create a more just and sustainable world. They also do this as a fiduciary responsibility to shareholders. It is my view that these businesses, their customers, and you the reader of this book, are on the cutting edge of a new era – that of the Caring Economy.

My three decades of public relations, crisis communications, and CSR work at leading brands have given me an insider's perspective which I am now sharing with you. I hope that my first-hand account of the evolution of CSR will help you become a more efficient and effective thought leader and doer inside your company, industry, and community.

From 2013 to 2016, I was able to launch a world-class CSR program for Christie's, the storied 250-year old auction house with annual sales of $7.4 billion. As Christie's first Chief CSR Officer, with just one direct report, two interns, and an annual budget of about $150,000, we were able to amplify Christie's position as the world's leading art business. Within three short years we were able to tell a compelling CSR story, supported with facts and figures. As noted in our 2015 Progress Report, across 43 countries we:

- Offset 2,380 metric tons of carbon emissions for all 9.4 million miles of corporate travel,
- Inaugurated a company-wide day of community service across the globe,
- Raised $4.4 million through online-only charity auctions,
- Raised $75.4 million with Christie's charity auctioneers, benefiting 300 charitable organizations globally,
- Raised $189 million for non-profit clients via our traditional sales calendar,
- Volunteered 4,086 hours of employee time in pro-bono services, and
- Supported 174 museum events globally.

These efforts also garnered us recognition from young recruits as well as the White House and the Mayor of London's office.[1]

Today, with the benefit of hindsight, I am able to apply Emerson's message about life to that of CSR – it is truly a journey not a destination. But we still must envision what the point of arrival looks like. As I have followed CSR's evolution, I have also concluded that businesses and their customers are launching us all into a Caring Economy, in which responsibility is critical for success. As you will see with this book, once you declare the start of your CSR journey, you will constantly uncover more layers and interconnections to an economy and a world that must be more compassionate, inclusive, and transparent. The consumers are willing this forward.

The rising consumer class of Millennials numbered 2 billion in 2017[2] according to the Pew Charitable Trust, and as they consume, they are sharing their experiences, learning from and supporting each other, and recognizing the fundamental importance of empathy and responsibility. From Parkland to Beijing to Saudi Arabia, they have an amplified voice through social media and are collectively willing forward a better future. This is a key foundation of our humanity and business leaders are tuning into it. They form the foundation of the Caring Economy and CSR is the essential channel for engaging them.

Building a CSR program from scratch

In 2011 my then-CEO at Christie's, Steven Murphy, asked me to develop a formal Corporate Social Responsibility department for the company. Over my previous 20 years in senior communications roles in multinational corporations, I had worked on countless CSR initiatives, but never before had I been formally given the full-time task of developing and implementing a CSR department. I was delighted to meet the particular challenge because of my belief in the need for companies to be responsible and to continually innovate.

I threw myself into the CSR role with drive, using my first year to conduct a listening tour with my colleagues and peers from other sectors to design a CSR program that would be a first and best-in-class in the art market. I had also just turned 50, a natural point of introspection. So, as I was reflecting on my own life, making meaning of my life story, I was also given to opportunity to lead my colleagues in a similar exercise for our 250-year old company. What did we stand for? What had we contributed? Where were we headed? Defining Christie's purpose and then sharing it with the world remains one of the most exciting challenges and accomplishments of my career.

We called our initiative Art + Soul. In the following years we developed a powerful and gratifying global volunteer program that engaged employees with disadvantaged youth in London, Hong Kong and New York to introduce them to art and culture. We used our auction house knowledge and resources to raise money for charitable causes. We engaged with dozens of cultural nonprofit organizations globally to create solutions to engaging the next generation of culture-seekers, not just wealthy art collectors. Along the way, we made our share of mistakes and learned from them. We measured our yearly results, put them in a formal report and used those results to drive us further.

Within the first year our global head of HR explained to me that the company wanted to formalize my role as head of CSR and switch my reporting line to the chief marketing officer. As head of corporate communications and CSR, I had always enjoyed direct access to the CEO and all of the other members of the executive suite. In that instant, I could see how by "elevating" CSR to a standalone function, Christie's had also relegated it – and me – to a subordinate role. The Art + Soul CSR program was effectively downgraded to just another one of Christie's several marketing initiatives.

It was both a painful personal realization and an important "Aha!" moment for me, one that led to the writing of this book. I continued at Christie's for another two years, so I could see clearly what had been possible before and after the CSR role had been moved to marketing. That day was the beginning of the end of effective CSR within that organization.

The silver lining in this moment was my deep conviction that CSR should be an expression of a brand's true purpose, guided from the top of the organization. Once Art + Soul was formalized as a marketing initiative, it lost a significant portion of its credibility and effectiveness. We still did plenty of worthwhile work, but we also passed on many other opportunities for truly meaningful CSR that failed to fit the marketing paradigm or capture the genuine engagement of the CEO.

It was this experience that has led to my belief that the goal of every CSR program is to seek its own end. And the more authentic the effort, the more competitive the company will be now and going forward. There is a point at which a company's responsibilities to society are so deeply aligned with its responsibilities to investors and employees that there is no meaningful distinction between business strategy and CSR strategy. At that point, smart business *is* CSR, and vice versa. Many companies are headed in this direction, and a few notable companies and business leaders have already arrived. You and your company could be next.

Seeking the triple-bottom-line

This book is meant to be a practical guide to building an effective and sustainable CSR platform within your organization. It shows examples of what true CSR success looks like and offers actionable insights into all the common pitfalls and distractions that can lead your CSR efforts astray. The model businesses showcased in the following pages demonstrate how the profit motive can go a long way toward innovating solutions that generate profits while also engaging social, environmental, and economic challenges.

In the past, if a business wanted to be good it would make a financial contribution to cheer shareholders or even employees – a charity donation here, a volunteer opportunity there. Those days are gone. Today profitable companies are learning that they must be attuned to the needs of the world's population in order to maximize profits and revenue growth.

CSR at its best is essentially a public accounting of a company's commitment to "the triple-bottom-line" – its people, its profitability, and the planet. Did we grow our people? Did we make money? Did we help or hurt the planet? This is the "triple-bottom-line" measurement of genuine success.

It evaluates the means a company uses to conduct business, not just the profits. The winning companies in a Caring Economy will succeed on the basis of this expanded bottom-line concept, while those that succeed with only one or two of the three face the risk of long-term decline.

The companies I have chosen to spotlight as models of CSR typically rank among the most admired companies in the world. Leaders at companies as diverse as Gucci, Tencent, Tesla, Lego, and Salesforce share with employees a higher corporate purpose than creating profitable transactions. These are companies that have aligned their profit-making missions with broader needs of their communities. For such purpose-driven organizations, CSR is the critical avenue through which each company's purpose gains expression.

In my career I have seen leaders who inspire their teams by their words followed by their actions – in all areas of their business, including CSR. I have been fortunate to learn from the best. Back in the 1990s, when I was with American Express, CEO Harvey Golub launched the SOS: Share Our Strength, program to combat hunger. By partnering with merchants in the dining sector, a critical market and revenue source for American Express, the company showed what was possible for CSR before it even called that. American Express took up the mantle of social responsibility in one of its areas of strength – where it could make the biggest impact, and also most fruitfully grow its brand reputation.

The rewards of having a purpose-driven focus are numerous and well documented. CSR offers an invaluable brand-building opportunity at a time when social media is making (and breaking) brands and brand-recognition more important than ever. CSR has also proven to be vital to employee engagement and retention. The Millennial generation (those born between roughly 1981 and 1997) now constitutes the largest adult demographic in history, and numerous surveys show Millennials have an overwhelming preference for employment at socially responsible companies. They are also among the large majority of consumers who say they are willing to pay more for sustainably produced goods and services. As older generations have passed along, the percentage of consumers who prefer sustainable goods has been climbing steadily. For makers of consumer products, CSR is a vital source of pricing power required for maintaining profitability.

10

In other words, a company that is socially responsible is a company built for long-term sustainable success. Throughout this book you will see the word "sustainability" used frequently as a synonym for social responsibility. Sustainability might be seen as the fulfillment of the promise of social responsibility. By taking socially responsible approaches in dealing with the company's many stakeholders (the planet included), management ensures that these stakeholder relationships are healthy and sustainable for the long term.

For these and other reasons, research shows that companies that embrace CSR are more successful than those that do not. Typically, sustainability goals for organizations are broken into three broad categories of concern: environmental, social, and governance, known as ESG. According to one Harvard study,[3] firms making investments and improving their performance on ESG issues exhibit better stock market performance and profitability in the future. These are profitable, mission-driven companies, with all employees informed and in support of that mission, addressing challenges to their communities and the planet.

The challenges facing the globe are enormous, so it is great news that addressing these challenges is also consistent with sustainable business success. We need more companies to engage in CSR. We need all hands on deck. The financial power of the marketplace is so immense that it is incumbent on every player within that marketplace to contribute to the cause of global peace, inclusion, and prosperity. Connectivity and globalization are offering both challenges and opportunities in the effort, and only businesses have the resources and talent to scale for impact.

Leaders of the profitable corporations in the Caring Economy will be those who understand that company stakeholders expect them to be socially responsible, transparent, and accountable. The studies suggest that management efforts to do good will be rewarded – by their customers, by loyal employees, and by also by investors, who are increasingly using CSR data to inform their investment decisions. If you can influence your company to fully embrace CSR, you are helping your company prevail in the long run. Through CSR, your company can grow as part of the solution, not part of the problem.

CSR as business discipline

The chapters in this book are arranged to take you through the entire journey of building a CSR program at your company, starting with your company's mission. An effective CSR program expresses your company's brand DNA, as experienced and reflected by employees, customers, suppliers, and business partners. Chapter one shows how to take the first steps in this direction, by setting some goals and objectives, researching what your company may be already doing well with CSR, and by identifying fellow employees willing to help with the company's CSR efforts.

In Chapter Two, it is time to develop your initial CSR strategies, and to build an informal sounding board as you proceed. Reaching out to CSR professionals at other companies offers valuable insights as to how there is no need to reinvent the wheel at the early stages of your effort.

Chapter Three looks at some of the best examples of corporate CSR projects. Practicing CSR successfully requires working from the inside out, from employees to customers to the planet. Your company must engage employees first before it can succeed at customer-facing CSR, and it must succeed at both before it can hope to affect change beyond. Companies that are authentically good citizens of the planet (and of their local communities) are almost always strong CSR practitioners at the employee level, and with the products and services they sell.

As you develop your CSR program, you will inevitably experience ups and downs with various projects, as well as occasional Aha! moments that signal new unforeseen opportunities. Chapter Four explores all the ways to deal with these challenges and opportunities, how to weather disappointments, and recognize the successes that open the door to creating a stronger and more impactful program.

One of the great breakthroughs for CSR in recent years is the rise of standardized measurements and benchmarks that allow your CSR's impact to be accurately evaluated and compared with peer organizations. Chapter Five helps you see where and how various measures of success can be used to show your progress, detect problem areas, rally employee support for CSR, and assure management that you are on the right track.

Chapter Six provides examples of how you can build on your successes to take your CSR program to new heights. The work of CSR is never done. It is an ongoing campaign. That is true for every company, even among the largest companies with the most advanced and sophisticated CSR programs. By its very nature, CSR needs to grow organically in response to changes in corporate leadership, corporate direction, and global challenges.

In the final chapter, which I have entitled Utopia, I show how CSR is destined to become integrated into common business practice, as one facet of a smart and sustainable overall business discipline. There is little need for a separate CSR function or office at any company where the mission and goals of the corporation are absolutely aligned with CSR-based objectives. CSR ends when everyone from the executive suite on down understands and embraces CSR values as the company's values. It ends when employee performance and compensation are assessed on a similar basis. It ends when everyone in the company exercises CSR reflexively each day because, for that company, social responsibility is synonymous with fiscal responsibility and sustainable long-term growth. This puts any brand ahead of its competitors and at the epicenter of the Caring Economy.

The Caring Economy

CSR practitioners, in my view, are privileged to be working at the very frontier of what spells business success for the coming decades. At its best, CSR is profitable, accountable, inclusive, empowering, and makes the world a better place. This is the new emerging business paradigm for the Caring Economy of the 21st Century.

Throughout this book, you will see notes of caution, however, regarding CSR at its worst. There are companies that continue to "greenwash" their bad behavior with charitable donations and marketing programs that cynically exploit the attractiveness of the CSR message. You will read about the infamous case of an oil company that spent a meager $5,000 to protect a rare butterfly species, but spent millions in television ads to brag about its good deed.

In this way, CSR risks becoming a cover for feel-good marketing – pure window-dressing to help enhance a company's financials without making an impact on the company's sustainability. CSR practitioners may also become seduced by CSR's natural appeal without recognizing that their colleagues are not truly engaged around it. Reality checks need to be built in along the CSR journey.

Without the triple-bottom-line woven into a company's business model, CSR's power is limited to that of traditional charity, if not mere window-dressing. That is truly CSR at its worst, an ostentatious, inauthentic display of caring meant to advance nothing except the company's narrow self-interest.

Traditionally, businesses distinctly focused on products and services while governments and not-for-profit organizations focused on making a better world. The two sat at opposite ends of the spectrum, mistrustful of one another. Today there are still elements in the corporate sector that ignore CSR and draw profits from human rights abuses, environmental degradation, and economic injustice. These are the bad actors that have long made corporations appear to be such unlikely sources for solving the world's problems.

I am glad to say that there are plenty of signs that the days are numbered for such companies. Threat-levels keep rising for companies that do business as usual and ignore their social responsibilities. Thanks to social media and growth of CSR monitoring and ratings agencies, companies that fail to grow their people and improve the planet will soon see those profits whither because no one will want to work for them or buy from them.

The latest wave is coming from the investment community. In January 2018, in his annual letter to corporate CEOs,[4] Laurence Fink, CEO of asset manager BlackRock, challenged companies to address the impact of significant political, economic, societal, and technological changes on their current strategies for long-term value creation: "As BlackRock engages with your company this year, we will be looking to see how your strategic framework reflects and recognizes the impact of the past year's changes in the global environment. How have these changes affected your strategy and how do you plan to pivot, if necessary, in light of the new world in which you are operating?"

Studies continue to show that companies ranking high in their ESG measurements for sustainability are more profitable over time. That is because a focus on the triple-bottom-line of people, profit, and planet carries a greatly reduced long-term business risk. Harvard Business School professor George Serafeim says that sustainability now ranks as the fastest-growing cause of shareholder activism. Literally trillions of dollars of investment capital are no longer available to the managers of companies with unsustainable business models, and those companies' stock prices are suffering as a result.

The exact opposite is true for truly great, sustainable brands. It is hardly a coincidence that Apple has become the world's first trillion-dollar company, in terms of market capitalization. At a shareholder meeting in 2015, Apple CEO Tim Cook was berated by an investor for wasting the company's money on environmental initiatives that contributed nothing to its profitability. Cook shot back, "We do a lot of things for reasons besides the profit motive."[5] Then he advised investors who were uncomfortable with Apple's pursuit of sustainability to go ahead and put their money elsewhere.[6] Between 2016 and 2018, Apple's stock more than doubled in value.

Soon it will be impossible to compete against such brands in a world that is increasingly connected and well-informed. Successful CSR practitioners who are capable of helping their companies deliver on the triple-bottom-line of people, planet, and profit will lead the way into this future. Stay the course. You will not be disappointed.

CHAPTER ONE
Great Brands Are Purpose Driven

"Be the change that you wish to see in the world."
– Mahatma Gandhi

At the 2013 TED conference, luxury fashion label Gucci launched Chime for Change (CFC), a global campaign for gender equality and empowerment for girls and women. Co-founders Beyoncé Knowles-Carter, and Salma Hayek Pinault led the event in traditional Gucci style, along with Gucci creative director Frida Giannini.

Through its crowdfunding partner Catapult, Chime for Change has created the first online platform that encourages people throughout the world to support girls' and women's projects in a personalized, individual way. Catapult connects Chime for Change community members directly to organizations and projects focused on the causes that matter most to them, representing over 50 organizations in 38 countries.

Chime for Change embraces a cause that resonates with Gucci's core client base: women with financial, social, and political influence. It is just one way Gucci has expressed its CSR purpose beyond its business focus on luxury goods and fashion design. As a powerful brand with global reach, Gucci has been able to set goals for its CSR initiatives that inspire a wide range of leading companies and organizations to pull in behind the effort.

Facebook, Hearst Magazines, and The Bill & Melinda Gates Foundation have all joined as strategic partners, with The Huffington Post serving as a digital media partner. An Advisory Board includes Archbishop Desmond Tutu and his daughter Mpho Tutu, John Legend, Jada Pinkett Smith, Julia Roberts, Meryl Streep, and many other issues experts, advocates and global leaders.

Most importantly, Gucci's CSR goals for gender equality have been endorsed from the start by Francois-Henri Pinault, chairman and CEO of Kering, Gucci's parent company, which calls itself "a global Luxury group." Pinault, husband of Salma Hayek

Pinault, said in a statement released for the CFC launch: "At [Kering], women form the majority of our employees as well as the majority of our customers. I hope that this initiative, shared with other individuals and organizations, will contribute to making a change for the better for women and their communities around the world...I am convinced that across the planet, women are at the heart of the equilibrium of our communities. There is a need to transform words into action and find new ways to enable and empower girls and women."[7]

1.1. Seek mission alignment

Support from the top is vital to the success of CSR at any organization, so the key to beginning and sustaining your CSR effort is to set goals and objectives that are very strongly aligned with the mission and business goals already embraced by the organization's leadership. In the case of Gucci, Chime for Change was just the latest incarnation of the company's long history of engagement with gender issues. "Women, for Gucci, as you can imagine, are very important," Gucci's President and CEO Marco Bizzarri told a Forbes interviewer in 2015. "Our objective is to link the visibility that we have as a brand worldwide and try to launch this initiative to help gender equality." Gucci also actively contributes toward UNICEF initiatives in support of girls' education.

Most brands with the greatest success in CSR have found that such alignment is a big help in tackling all of the most commonly cited obstacles to CSR success: engaging employees, identifying partners, finding funding, staffing programs, and tracking and measuring results.

"With so many good causes out there in the world, our biggest obstacle with CSR was identifying focus areas that were best suited to our capabilities and would drive the greatest global impact," says Tae Yoo, the senior vice president who stewards CSR for Cisco, the $49 billion technology conglomerate. "We've been able to do this by articulating a clear strategy that is aligned with our core competencies. We are a global tech company and believe technology is an equalizer in creating a sustainable, inclusive world. Therefore, our CSR efforts are applied towards supporting programs, entrepreneurs, and organizations that leverage technology to help solve some of the world's biggest problems."

Cisco is an exceptional company in this respect. Too often, CSR is executed in an ad hoc, nonintegrated fashion. One case is the Ford Motor Company Fund's donations for breast cancer research, totaling $136 million since 1993. There is no argument that breast cancer research is an eminently worthy cause, but there is also no strategic link between medical research and the building of cars and trucks. As a practical matter, a company in the auto industry can leverage much more philanthropic impact by exercising CSR along the lines of its key competencies in transportation design, engineering, manufacturing, distribution, and marketing.

Ford has faced some very difficult times over the past 25 years. In 2018 Wall Street analysts downgraded its stock because the company has fallen behind its peers in emerging automotive technologies. Perhaps Ford would be in a better market position today if, over the past two decades, it had funded more activities within strategically aligned CSR causes such as fuel economy, emissions control, electric drivetrains, and CSR standards for suppliers and materials recycling. The results of such initiatives may well have led to innovative new automotive technologies, new products, and new revenue streams. Also, Ford would be better positioned to enhance employee engagement within the company if it had funded a leadership role for itself in industry-specific CSR issues such as carbon footprint, environmental sustainability, and responsible supply-chain management.

Decision makers within every company commonly make calculations as to whether a new product or sales campaign will reflect the brand's innate qualities and build on the brand's reputation. Ideally, objective-setting for CSR should be undertaken with this same level of brand discipline. At many of the best brands in the world this alignment between brand objectives and CSR objectives is fairly clear, as shown in the chart below.

Examples of Brands Aligning CSR Objectives with Business Practices

Company	Industry	Sample of CSR Objectives
Tata	Manufacturing	Tata's CSR program, STRIVE, equips communities in India with information, technology, and other resources to help improve their health, education, and livelihood outcomes.
Disney	Entertainment	Disney's CSR mainly focuses on reducing the negative environmental impacts of its operations and supporting international standards for labor practices and responsible supply chain management. The company also funds wildlife conservation, charitable giving, and employee volunteerism.
Target	Retail	Target puts aside 5% of its profit for community giving, which adds up to $4 million each week. Target employees volunteer hundreds of thousands of hours in their communities every year.
American Express	Financial Services	Amex provides grants to local and national organizations, for community service, historic preservation, and adult leadership training.

Company	Industry	Sample of CSR Objectives
Tencent	E-commerce	With each new product and invention, Tencent strives to embrace philanthropy, expand the Internet, and be a model for all corporations who strive to improve our world through technology. In 2015 it launched 9/9 Charity Day, using its social media platform to raise millions of dollars for hundreds of non-profit organizations, with millions of users volunteering for public service.

Each of these companies pursues CSR in ways that are highly relevant to its industry, its customers, and their communities. Target, as a retailer, returns a portion of its profits to the communities that support its stores. American Express turns its financial expertise toward philanthropic grant-making. Tata, the largest manufacturer in India, applies its world-class technical know-how toward the improvement of poverty-stricken communities. Disney, with its vast international theme park and cruise line operations, sets its CSR sights on wildlife conservation, environmental sustainability, and fair labor practices. Tencent owns WeChat, the largest social media platform in China with over one billion subscribers. In 2015 the company launched its 9/9 Charity Day to generate millions of dollars and volunteer hours in support of charities every September.

How do you get your arms around the vast number of social and environmental needs in the world? The United Nations has a list of 17 Sustainable Development Goals, known as SDGs. These are universally understood, desirable objectives for achieving improved conditions for health, education, nutrition, climate, infrastructure and much more. It is in essence a catalogue of where all meaningful advocacy work is currently being done, and it can be an excellent reference tool for helping you define, expand, and focus the scope of your CSR platform.

"Five years ago, not many CEOs talked about the SDGs," says Rangu Salgame, CEO and founder of Princeton Growth Ventures, and formerly with Tata Communications. "In the last 12 months, it seems like almost all CEOs are talking about them. They are internalizing them into their business models."

Source:
https://www.un.org/sustainabledevelopment/news/communications-material/

1.2. Assess Your Existing CSR for Quick Wins

Starting down this path begins with picking what I would call the low-hanging fruit along the way. CSR initiatives can originate in all parts of an organization. Philanthropy is often directed by the personal preferences of the CEO, or the CEO's spouse. Corporate giving and employee volunteer activities are also commonly driven by highly motivated employees with pet causes, or by local charities that are adept at asking for help. If you were to map out your company's current giving and volunteer practices, you might discover that some do not align very well (or at all) with your company's mission, its customers, or where the company's expertise lay. All of those considerations point to areas of opportunity for CSR. They may even point to areas that will allow you to leapfrog beyond your competition in the minds of consumers.

Many companies that do not have CSR programs nonetheless exercise social responsibility by other names, by sharing their expertise on a philanthropic basis. At Christie's, for example, trained and highly qualified charity auctioneers regularly volunteer their personal time after work hours to conduct fundraising auctions for all sorts of organizations and causes, including poverty, cancer research, education and humanitarian relief. Most professional service firms provide pro bono legal, financial and strategic planning consulting to non-profit organizations. Activities of this kind can become an important part of your company's overall CSR program. If some parts of the organization are already doing it, then you have a practical model for how other parts can begin participating under the CSR banner.

A simple internal discovery process will likely reveal other areas of your organization where CSR is already being practiced, related to their respective functions. For example, many professional organizations and trade groups have established goals and objectives that represent CSR best practices for Human Resources, Finance, Operations, and other areas. By taking a department-by-department inventory, you can get a sense of the direction your company is already headed with regards to CSR. It is here that you are also likely to find your first CSR allies and champions among your colleagues.

Government regulatory reporting offers another perspective on your company's current CSR profile. Most companies, for example, already file regular reports on air emissions as a matter of environmental compliance. There are similar filings for worker safety with OSHA, equal opportunity practices under EEOC, and disabled access in ADA compliance. Tax filings document the corporate philanthropy record.

Most of this information is already available online via company websites as a matter of public disclosure. That is true of your industry rivals and competitors, as well. Google "CSR" with the names of your top three competitors and you will see what your competitors are (and aren not) doing. More importantly, you will see what is being said about them by their customers, investors, and other important stakeholders. Dig a little deeper through LinkedIn, Facebook, Instagram, WeChat, and other social networks, and you are likely to gather even richer insight into how your competition is faring on CSR.

A little desktop research of this kind can give your CSR effort a tremendous jumpstart. You should compile the results of your findings in a fairly simple checklist that catalogues potential areas for CSR activities.

One reliable resource to consult as you begin is The Global Reporting Initiative (GRI), an independent international standards organization that helps businesses, governments, and other organizations take stock of their CSR impact. A second resource tailored for investors is the Sustainability Accounting Standards Board (SASB), a U.S.-based non-profit that develops and promotes accounting standards for sustainability, much like FASB (the Financial Accounting Standards Board) promotes accounting principles for financial reporting.

GRI and SASB will be discussed in greater detail in Chapter 5 when it is time to measure CSR results. These measurement tools are equally valuable at the start of the CSR journey, because they can help you set your objectives. Both GRI and SASB also provide comprehensive resources to help identify the areas by which an organization can gauge its performance for CSR in terms of the triple-bottom-line. Their tools will help you answer questions about how your company defines and measures its CSR efforts.

The triple-bottom-line is the most common accounting framework being used by businesses to assess CSR performance. The triple-bottom-line method asks you to see beyond your organization's traditional financial bottom line by gauging you social and environmental impact, as well. Measuring your business using the triple-bottom-line is one of the best ways to evaluate the sustainability of your business, how profitable it really is, and how it can best maintain its future growth.

SASB's many online resources can be very helpful in early stages of your CSR efforts, thanks to SASB's emphasis on targeting the most relevant sustainability issues within specific industries. SASB's recommended early steps can help you:

- Identify aspects of your company's performance that impact society.
- Define the most relevant information that can be reasonably collected.
- Present the data in a standardized format that allows comparison of relative performance.

These kinds of resources from SASB and GRI may seem a little overwhelming at first. GRI, in particular, is too complex for most companies and is most useful for highly regulated publicly traded companies. In the early going, it is valuable to look carefully at your company and its peers in order to decide the depth of CSR measurement that is most worthwhile. "Measure what is material to your business and your stakeholders," is the advice I was given by Andrea Sullivan, Head of International Environment, Social & Governance for Bank of America Merrill Lynch.

Consider approaching all these checklists and benchmarks the way you would a menu at a restaurant you are visiting for the first time. You cannot possibly order everything at once, but certain menu items will appeal to your appetite. SASB and GRI will provoke your thinking and help you identify objectives that are more likely to provide a good fit with your organization. The SASB perspective is that its takes a limited number of key performance indicators in order to contribute to a balanced reporting regime – one that serves the dual demands of comprehensiveness and practicability.

1.3. Make your SWOT Analysis: Strengths, Weaknesses, Opportunities, and Threats

Another very practical way to shake out your short-term triple-bottom-line points of emphasis is to undertake a standard SWOT analysis: strengths, weaknesses, opportunities, and threats.

- Which items represent your company's strengths, where brand alignment might make a powerful statement? Think of Intel's use of its technology to empower more people to innovate and harnessing its data to address society's most complex issues – from climate change to energy efficiency to economic empowerment and human rights. Also consider which of the United Nations' 17 Sustainable Development Goals, the SDGs, are most relevant to your company and its customers.

- Which items represent some of your company's weaknesses and vulnerabilities, where attention needs to be paid to avoid potential problems with customers and other stakeholders? Think of how the Nike and Apple brands suffered due to years of inattention regarding the way their overseas suppliers were treating low-wage workers.

- Which items represent clear opportunities, where positive action is most likely to attract employee engagement, leverage the capabilities of company suppliers, and attract strategic partners outside the organization? Think of Tata's technical assistance to poor communities and the way American Express contributes its financial wizardry to its philanthropic partnerships.

- Which items represent areas of threat to the organization, where a lack of CSR attention in a particular area might put the company at a serious competitive disadvantage? Think of how small startup companies such as Honest and Method took on Procter & Gamble and other consumer product giants with distinctive CSR messages that were central to their brand appeal. Could your organization become a victim of this kind of disruptive competitor?

As you consider your potential CSR objectives, give some thought to how they will enable you to generate measurable outcomes you can report on later. The retailer Target provides an excellent example of how a major firm is able to report on its practical and understandable CSR accomplishments in an attractive and easy-to-understand way.

Target's CSR is branded internally as "Future at Heart" with four broad areas of focus: Empower Teams (equal pay and diversity hiring), Serve Guests (sustainable products and services), Foster Communities (corporate philanthropy), and Design Tomorrow (sustainable operations).[8] The company's 2018 CSR report details goals for 2020 in all four areas (including a $15 hourly minimum wage and 100% renewable energy use) and significant achievements towards those goals.

The entire presentation is consistent and aligned with Target's overall brand message. Its simplicity and relevance help burnish the Target brand among a wide range of stakeholders: consumers, employees, investors, suppliers, media, and government.

1.4. Go on a listening tour

All this early research and analysis will pay off later when you need to make a case for CSR funding and other resources with your organization's top decision-makers. The important thing in this phase is to not get ahead of yourself and try to do too much before getting more people involved. By starting small and scaling up, you will have more chances to engage your colleagues in CSR work. A broad base of support among employees is crucial in persuading management that a sustained commitment to CSR is both the right thing to do and the smart thing to do. I remember one of my sounding board peers at Hershey telling me that when it comes to

CSR, "Management never knows what it wants but will like what you get."

My experience suggests that the best CSR programs begin with internal dialogue about what success might look like for the company and its brand. You might start the discussions by noting the three most important agreed-upon goals for the company, and then gauge the level of employee interest in CSR objectives aligned with those goals. CSR leadership entails reconciling your company's vision and mission with the CSR activities that will resonate best with your company's employees.

At Christie's we began our CSR journey with a series of brainstorming sessions at a representative set of locations where the auction house operates. I conducted sessions often as a complement to management offsite sessions, where CSR was just one of many agenda items during the meetings. I held countless in-person meetings, teleconferences, and email exchanges with colleagues across ranks and geographies to foster an ongoing dialogue about what CSR might look like at Christie's. I did a six-month listening tour, meeting with individuals, small groups, and ultimately with a global town hall. From New York to London to Hong Kong to Paris, via conference calls and in-person meetings, we tried to engage with as many employees as possible.

I used the global listening tour as a means to test-drive certain concepts and to infuse the company with a commonly shared definition of what CSR is and what it might look like (or not) for us. For example, we discussed environmental issues and our carbon footprint – Christie's staff fly frequently on business and the company prints tons of catalogues for its sales. We also looked at philanthropic funds and the possibility of setting up a foundation or grants program. We looked at the role of volunteerism in terms of employee development and engagement. We spent considerable time looking at our corporate mission as it related to our CSR. For 250 years Christie's has been the convener of buyers and sellers of great works of art, and done so with a greater degree of transparency and accountability than any other leader in the commercial art market. We ultimately agreed that a key part of our CSR mission is to steward great works of art from one caregiver to the next.

This exercise was foundational for our objective setting and also made it much smoother to implement our CSR activities when we launched them. In a sense, we had primed the pump. It certainly helps that many Christie's employees are drawn to the business for its aesthetic and educational values, so the non-commercial nature of CSR activities resonates with them.

As you roll out your offsite sessions, also try to co-host them with department or division heads who oversee the groups you are meeting. You can partner with them ahead of time to allow for efficient use of time and consistent message delivery during your sessions. They will most likely see you as an ally once you familiarize them with CSR and your objectives. Let them know from the start that you are not asking them for funds or headcount but actually spiritual support in making the company even greater and its employees even more inspired. They will see this as an easy lift that also allows them to shine.

Interestingly for us, at every session that I facilitated, the reception from employees ranged from neutral to very positive. There was no negative reaction. In fact, the majority of employees were actually hungry for CSR or something CSR-like. And you do not need to overthink it or overanalyze it because as a general phenomenon, most stakeholders will welcome your efforts and give you the benefit of the doubt in making an effort toward greater responsibility so long as it does not tax them too much. In all my years leading Christie's CSR, I never had a single media query challenging our reporting or internal detractors who disagreed with our efforts.

Building a CSR platform involves a mix of "tenacity and finesse" says Andrea Sullivan. People want to be engaged but you need to find what resonates for them. She adds,"It's helping colleagues to see the relevance of CSR in their role and to bring them on the company's journey."

1.5. Define your terms.

In smaller meetings, I would usually open by inquiring what each person's knowledge of CSR was so that I could tailor our time together for efficiency and effectiveness. This was early 2013, so CSR was still fairly new to most companies that were not multinational or publicly traded. Most colleagues had limited if any knowledge about CSR by name, or the term was mixed up in their experience with terms such as sustainability or corporate citizenship.

Also, words mean different things in different cultures. During these discussions in Europe, for instance, I learned that use of the term "sustainability" is normally limited to environmental matters, and not associated with social and governance practices. So when I spoke of sustainability in broader terms, pertaining to Christie's long-term health as a socially responsible company, my European colleagues were likely to misunderstand me.

My advice then and now has always been to get out on the table the various concepts that CSR may connote for colleagues, and never assume that everyone sees CSR the same way. This gives you a sense of your colleagues' preconceived notions about CSR and helps guide you in engaging them in it. You get a sense of what you may be up against, as well as where you have informed and willing supporters.

While it is important to agree upon certain defined terms, it is also important to not get hung up on semantics or specifics in these early meeting. Keep in mind that aim of the program is to be a more responsible company. With this as your North Star, it is very hard to be thwarted or confused. It is also an opportunity to compliment your colleagues because they are collaborating on making your organization even greater.

Though you are unlikely to face negativity in these discussions, you will often run into some level of skepticism. Skeptics may accuse you of 'greenwashing' or undertaking CSR simply for public relations. Anticipate such an accusation and prepare your answer. If you sense that your CSR is going to be an extension of marketing and not independent, then rethink how you are approaching it. It will not endure if it is not genuine and additive to your community and clients as well as your bottom line. Research online what your competition has or has not done and how you are even better at it. Ask your employees what resonates as authentic and what does not. They will help you shape the best answers and be your best advocates once they are vested in your CSR by you.

Money and time will likely be among the most commonly debated topics because there is never enough of either. The airing of these kinds of concerns is a healthy process, so it is important to learn to welcome bumps and roadblocks along the way. The best response to steer the conversation toward CSR approaches that work within existing budgets and activities. You are not asking them specifically for budget or even staff time during working hours. Simply invite them to think of your initiative more like a pilot program that can scale up with success, and that your intention is to cast your colleagues and their teams as heroes in your corporate narrative. In my experience, it is nearly impossible for a business leader to oppose such a proposition.

By the time you have conducted three or four sessions, you will find that you are prepared to address just about any employee concern, in just about any region or function. And once you resolve issues with select colleagues, you will begin to see the resistance can usually be bucketed into a handful of categories such as funding or staff time. Any lingering fears and suspicions you might find are most reliably quelled by the reminder that CSR works best when employees are the heroes of the narrative – and that your commitment is to that particular result. I have found that with some people who may have anxiety over who gets the credit, this reassurance goes a long way toward garnering their support.

Interpersonal issues can be addressed on a smaller scale through workshops. For workshops I recommend having three formats for engagement. Have a half-day, one-hour, and three-minute exercise that you can conduct regularly based on what your audience can give you. If a department head can give you the time at their offsite, jump at the chance to fill half of a day or an hour at least. The half-day option will allow for breakout sessions where colleagues can internalize and brainstorm ways to activate CSR. An hour session can do the same, although maybe without the breakout sessions. The three-minute option is super easy to deploy in elevators or dropping by someone's office, work station or weekly meeting. And a time-tested secret for getting people's attention is to feed them. The offer of cookies, candy, bagels or just about anything ingestible will help ensure increased attendance.

Listening tours have always served me well, and I rely on them as a vital early stage of any major effort, including the development of a CSR platform. A cardinal rule of communications is to know one's audience and the listening tour facilitates defining and understanding the audience more fully. I consult with colleagues, clients, customers, and business partners to share my ideas and solicit their comments and suggestions. The added benefit is that it lays the initial foundation for future dialogue and pulse-taking as one rolls out an initiative, allowing the proponent to create a stronger, more relevant, and tested solution for any challenge at hand.

1.6. Create a CSR culture

Within pilot projects and confidential deals at Christie's, we used code names. For the start of our CSR journey we came up with the codename of Art + Soul, and colleagues quickly noted that the name perfectly expressed what our entire CSR program stood for. As I work-shopped the idea with my colleagues globally, a consensus around the name solidified, probably around the third or fourth session. One of our first accomplishments as a CSR program was to agree on a name we could rally around. We had created something seemingly from nothing, and Art + Soul rapidly became an essential part of Christie's company culture.

Catherine Mathis, my former boss at The New York Times Company, used to say that great brands are built from the inside out. Her point was that when leadership encourages employees to exercise their brand's values inside the company, customers, and external stakeholders will get the brand message loud and clear. The great companies that I have worked with generally have employees who share a common sense of purpose, which is a key determinant of each company's level of success. CSR works best when it is aligned with that purpose and can contribute to strengthening the company's culture. Art + Soul expresses Christie's brand values through socially responsible activities.

Studies by executive recruitment firm Korn Ferry have shown organizations can improve overall employee engagement and performance by using their CSR agenda as a leadership development tool. "Tapping into an organization's social responsibility platform is critically important to attracting, developing and retaining top talent," says Noah Rabinowitz of the leadership development practice at Hay Group, a Korn Ferry division. "It provides a source of natural inspiration for people that is tied to the broader mission and purpose of an organization."[9]

Korn Ferry has found that CSR is generally underutilized for this purpose, but that the need for change is acute. The firm's 2016 global research report showed that engagement levels are lower than expected across all levels of leadership and that an average of only 36% of organizational talent is "highly engaged." The top factor that improves people's feelings about their job is working for a company whose culture aligns with their values, and this is especially true for younger Generation X and Millennial workers.

Most organizational leaders place talent retention among their top concerns, so it is worthwhile to share these and other survey data points when you discuss the benefits of CSR with your management. It is no coincidence that companies who rank among CSR trailblazers are also leaders in recruiting and developing employees that share their sense of purpose, as expressed through corporate mission and values. Great brands have always invested in their employees and then encouraged and supported those employees to get involved in industry associations and local communities. It is an effective way of spreading a brand message, and CSR makes the message even stronger.

By workshopping our program name globally, we were able to legitimize and normalize Art + Soul within Christie's culture. The name arose in such an organic way that I felt comfortable in presenting it to the CEO as a matter of fact. It was a way of putting a stake in the ground, and a big step for our company culture.

In my own experience, however, I have also seen that management's consent for CSR is not quite the same as management's embrace. This is a theme I will return to later. It is important to challenge yourself and your CSR colleagues to find ways to engage your organization's leaders in the program. You need to "manage up" and get top executives involved and invested. You will need to challenge them at times to help develop initiatives with you and to attend your volunteer outings. Even if they indicate they do not appreciate CSR's potential for helping the company succeed, leave open the option for them to grow toward CSR over time. For CSR to be sustainable within the organization, never give up on seeking top management's embrace.

CSR Beginner's Checklist

<u>Mission Alignment:</u> Get support from the top. Set your initial goals and objectives so they are strongly aligned with the mission and business goals already embraced by the organization's leadership.

<u>Quick Wins:</u> Pick the low-hanging fruit. Identify existing efforts and fold them into your CSR story.

<u>SWOT Analysis:</u> Plan your efforts based on your analysis of your organization's strengths, weaknesses, opportunities, and threats.

<u>Term Definitions:</u> From the start, get out on the table the various concepts that CSR may connote for colleagues, and never assume that everyone sees CSR the same way.

<u>Listening Tour:</u> Test market your thoughts with colleagues and listen for feedback and fresh perspectives. All this early research and analysis will pay off later when you need to make a case for CSR funding and other resources with your organization's top decision-makers.

<u>Company Culture:</u> Seek CSR opportunities that are best aligned with the company's culture and can contribute to strengthening it. Look for socially responsible initiatives that express your organization's agreed-upon brand values.

CHAPTER TWO
Building your CSR Platform

"A strategy delineates a territory in which
a company seeks to be unique."
– Michael Porter

In February 2015, the London-based consultancy Brand Finance announced that Danish toymaker LEGO had displaced Ferrari as number one in its annual ranking of "The World's Most Powerful Brands." Brand Finance lauded LEGO for its broad cross-generational appeal, customer loyalty, staff satisfaction, and strong corporate reputation.

LEGO's distinction as the world's most powerful brand, capped a decade-long turnaround. As recently as 2004, LEGO's parent company had been in deep trouble, hovering near bankruptcy, and reportedly losing $1 million per day. It was loaded with debt and saddled with too many money-losing product lines. A new CEO entered in 2005 and made many long-overdue moves to improve the company's balance sheet and change the company culture.

One important way LEGO sought to "restore the company's soul" was implementing something called the LEGO Brand Framework. In part, the framework defined how LEGO employees would fulfill the company's mission through three ambitious ESG objectives:

- Environment: "LEGO aims to lead on environmental performance in the toy industry and aspire to make our impact on the environment a positive one."
- Social: "Children are always LEGO's first priority. LEGO aims to make a global difference to child learning through play, to product safety in the toy industry, and to business behavior that promotes children's rights."
- Governance: "LEGO wants to uphold its long-standing values and caring culture and to promote high standards through transparent and ethical business practice."

These three ESG objectives gave birth to a series of strategic initiatives:

- Adopt a zero-waste mindset, using reground material and waste LEGO bricks in manufacturing.
- Invest in renewable energy and efficiency toward becoming carbon-neutral.
- Deliver play experiences with the highest safety standards.
- Eliminate product recalls.
- Expand local LEGO Community Engagement activities.
- Support development and learning for millions of children through the LEGO Group and the LEGO Foundation.
- Boost the level of female leaders.
- Develop world-class levels of employee safety.

These initiatives have been crucial in LEGO's turnaround by integrating CSR directly into its business operations. By 2015, 43% of appointed and recruited leaders within the company were female, a 20-point improvement over 2009. Also in 2015, LEGO made 175 million LEGO bricks from previously discarded waste bricks, and grew its commitment to community engagement. These strategies demonstrate how successful businesses are doing well by doing good.

You and your company can take a page of the LEGO playbook by working to interpret your company's mission statement and business goals through a similar CSR lens. What are the promises your company is already committed to, implied by its mission statement, that can give birth to CSR strategies? Within the organization's current strategic plan, where are there opportunities for CSR strategies to play a contributing role? What are the Human Resources department goals for health, safety, and diversity, and how can CSR help support and promote achievement of those goals? Which activities in your employees' lives and communities dovetail with your business strategies, products and services, thereby creating a natural opportunity to establish greater bonds with your stakeholders?

These are the types of CSR approaches that helped LEGO outperform the iconic Ferrari brand in customer loyalty, staff satisfaction, and corporate reputation. If a toy company can do it, any company can. CSR is not a hobby; it is a powerful business differentiator.

2.1. Building consensus and support

Adam Werbach, one-time head of the Sierra Club, has said that a fully imagined and implemented sustainability program can contribute three major strategies to an organization: "a bottom-line strategy to save costs, a top-line strategy to reach a new consumer base, and a talent strategy to get, keep, and develop creative employees." Those three concepts – bottom-line, top-line, and talent – each correspond somewhat closely to the ESG elements of environment, social, and governance.

Communicating, advancing, and reinforcing the opportunities that CSR strategies represent for your company is one of your first challenges in cultivating a CSR culture. I discovered that the most valuable by-product of the Christie's listening tour described in Chapter One was a company-wide network of contacts sympathetic to the cause. I came to call this group my internal sounding board, made up of people I could rely on for dialogue and pulse-taking as our plans and initiatives rolled out. It was a true mosaic of colleagues not necessarily defined by title, tenure or talent, per se, but by these colleagues' shared desire to foster a larger sense of community – a community that not only transcended their immediate role, department or location, but a community to reached beyond pure business lines.

Your CSR program, in effect, should become a brand within the organization if it is going to succeed and grow. So it is helpful to follow four keys of branding success, as outlined by the Interbrand consulting group: clarity, commitment, responsiveness, and governance.

A. Be clear about what CSR means for your organization.

It will be difficult to communicate it effectively to your colleagues until you have developed your own depth of understanding in this regard and can express it fluently. I had an edge in this respect as a career communications professional. I was prepared to write succinctly about CSR in terms that I thought would make my colleagues intrigued and receptive to the message. And I was schooled in reconciling business goals with the goals of others – journalists, bloggers, investors, and employees. If persuasive writing of this kind is not a particular strength of yours, see if you can get help from the communications department within your organization. It helps to define CSR as a brand launch, developed from research you have done on your listening tour.

At first glance, very few people are likely to appreciate the cost-saving, market-building, and talent retention possibilities that CSR can bring to the organization. Gaining clarity about these possibilities early on can really help your CSR program take off. Then sharing examples of what success looks like with other brands can help drive home your message.

In my experience, many people still interpret CSR as an environmental practice involving "greening" your company. It is also common for people to interpret the social component of CSR as charitable giving (when it can be so much more) and then fail to see any obvious CSR relationship with company governance.

You may find colleagues politely nodding knowingly when you engage them around CSR but be sure to repeat your messages and question them about their views and how CSR might apply to them and their roles. When they give you their interpretation and application of CSR to their work, listen for the discrepancies with your own view, and keep asking questions. Early misunderstandings can be beneficial if you use them to build a dialogue around closing that gap, and thereby build greater engagement with your colleagues.

For instance, in the early days of our CSR roll-out at Christie's, I regularly explained that although the environment was important to our Art + Soul project, office-paper recycling was not nearly as critical an activity as leveraging our unique auctioneering skills to fundraise for not-for-profits – particularly those not-for-profit organizations that mattered most to our top clients. It broadened everyone's thinking about the possibilities of CSR when I was able to show how Christie's unique competencies could leverage much more socially beneficial activity than mere corporate giving.

And it mattered even more when we began to track those sales results and report on them. I would periodically amuse colleagues needing convincing of an old quotation often attributed to former GE CEO Jack Welch: "In God we trust; all others bring data." In year one of Art + Soul, the "look of success" with auctioneering activities supporting charitable causes was more than $250 million. Finally we were taking credit for something we had been doing all along.

So it is important from the start to define CSR for your organization in all the ways that your organization affects society and can best contribute to society (The broadest and most holistic definitions of CSR have the added virtue of being more inclusive and inspiring). In your written communications, one sure way of unlocking the power of language is to anticipate the concerns of skeptics and naysayers and address them with positive examples of concrete success stories from leading brands, including the ones I have cited elsewhere in the book.

Another sound practice that ensures accuracy is creating a FAQ – a Frequently Asked Questions sheet – where you can put all the questions or issues that come to mind as you write. In filling out the FAQ, you will inevitably find places where your answers are lacking in persuasive details. Even if you don't have all the answers right away, the first-draft of your FAQ will give you a handy basis of discussion with colleagues in all the key functional areas that are key to CSR success, such as Human Resources, Communications, Marketing, and Operations. The FAQ also becomes your institutional knowledge around CSR so that others can tap into it if or when you are not in their time zone or functional area. In a sense, the FAQ allows you to scale up your CSR when budgets and headcount caps would not otherwise allow you to spread your CSR gospel. And any feedback you get around your FAQ can only make your CSR program battle tested and stronger, which is ideal for any ongoing campaign.

To that end, all along the way, you will stimulate feedback via events, written communications and other ways, and you can factor it into your written documents and your presentations to your colleagues. Your communications pitch for CSR will grow stronger each time that you deliver it and hear from your employees. This campaign mentality never really goes away, nor should it. As the CSR platform launches and develops, you will need to remain in campaign mode, always reaching out, creating new initiatives, and delivering updates to attract still more momentum for CSR.

B. Demonstrate and communicate your commitment.

Your colleagues were plenty busy before CSR came along, so you have to demonstrate the commitment that assures them CSR is for real, and that it is here to stay. Any effort that shows evidence of inadequate commitment runs the risk of losing their attention – after which they will lose their faith in you and your program.

Begin with the little things that demonstrate commitment. Do not launch a blog unless you are ready to keep it fresh and up-to-date. If there are materials to distribute in the workplace, make sure they do not hang around on bulletin boards and other places past their due dates. No matter how much you as the CSR leader feels committed, you must be aware of any inadvertent signals you are giving that might lead people to assume CSR at the company is just a passing fad or somebody else's job. Maybe informal brainstorms around the water cooler or in the company cafeteria will garner more insight than an all-staff email? Test different ways to demonstrate commitment to true employee dialogue. Most workplaces have seen good ideas come and go, and it is up to you to demonstrate that this is not the case with CSR.

CSR grows and thrives with strong internal communications that informs everyone in the company of all the good work being done on sustainability issues. Unfortunately, CSR communications is typically under-resourced, and in companies where the CSR point person is not a communications professional, that can be a problem.

"I would say the biggest hurdle that our customers face in procurement roles is that they're not communications professionals," says Jennifer Beason, head of communications, SAP Corporate Social Responsibility. SAP Ariba, an SAP subsidiary, is the world's largest business-to-business network, connecting more than 3.4 million buyers and sellers in 190 countries. Many people working in finance and procurement are making large, impactful buying decisions that support sustainable products and businesses, but the news is not being communicated to the rest of their companies. "These are new jobs that need to be created," says Beason. "Internal communication is essential for digital transformation to occur in companies."

Digital communications are the way of the world and you can use them to your advantage, both to save costs and to generate fresh content on your activities. See if your Human Resources, Corporate Communications or Investor Relations department create regular communications where you could plug into their existing communications channels and calendars. This step may be necessary anyway, if CSR communications are under the signature of your CEO or another C-level executive.

In some instances, you will have to draft the full communication yourself, but in the early going, it is wise to find a willing volunteer embedded within the HR or Communications team that would welcome the opportunity to help you with the campaign. CSR is by nature highly motivational and idealistic, so the substance of particular efforts tends to be far more interesting and engaging that most other corporate communications. If you can identify supporters and volunteers willing to help with these chores, you build credibility for the program while making your life easier and the CSR roll-out more effective.

As you begin to map your specific CSR strategies, building and maintaining this network becomes your most important everyday task. You want to connect with people who believe in a CSR – and what is in essence a broader sense of community and caring – and then support them, encourage them and develop some of them as your super-volunteers.

I am sure you can already begin to think of colleagues in your organization who are primed to receive your CSR message. Who are the ones who organize bake sales and blood drives? Who are the ones who are almost maniacal about recycling? Who are the ones who run in breast cancer runs and walk in the AIDS walk? Who teaches Sunday school or is a den mother for Boy Scouts? If you begin to consider your colleagues through a different lens – a lens of service or civic engagement – then you will be tuning into a wealth of potential CSR champions. Start to list their names for future reference.

In the effort to engage more senior colleagues, do your best to make it easy for them to help carry the CSR banner. One way is to offer to co-present CSR with a senior manager at one of their team meetings. If you feel reluctant to ask, consider that leaders are always looking for fresh ways to engage their teams and inspire them to rise to the next level. Practicing CSR can be a hands-on way of personalizing and operationalizing this competitive advantage and developing leadership skills. If you work with senior managers to see how CSR activities can lend fuel to their team's success, they will see CSR as a valuable instrument and you as a valuable ally. As well, in organizations where job promotions and salary raises are more limited, involving employees in CSR activities allows them to grow professionally and be recognized for their leadership capabilities.

Try to show senior managers various ways to link CSR to the annual review process. The employee goal setting process that occurs with annual reviews is an opportune time for managers to create CSR-supportive goals that will advance the business. Managers have a limited number of initiatives and positions that they can use when coaching their teams. CSR is an additional tool in that coaching toolbox. You may find a benefits administrator in your Human Resources department willing to lead the charge toward digital signatures and record keeping in an effort to save paper, process more efficiently, and demonstrate his or her leadership skills.

Ask yourself if your CSR audiences are demographically representative and engaged with your presentations. If the answer is "no," consider asking your CEO to help rally the troops – they may need a signal from the top that the company supports their participation. You will find CSR ambassadors throughout your company if you continue to experiment with ways of meeting them where they are and aligning CSR strategies with theirs. Perhaps there is a middle manager in your sales team who is inspired to rally his department for an annual volunteer outing. Any exercise, no matter is scale or success, is additive to your end goal of integrating CSR into your business.

Another opportunity to tap into is the wealth of professional associations and online tools dedicated to CSR. From the IABC (the International Association of Business Communicators) to the 3BL and CSR newswire, to the Center for Corporate Citizenship at Boston College to CSR and the Law, there is a wealth of knowledge and inspiration for you to tap into – literally at your fingertips. Simply Googling "CSR Resources" will provide you with some of the most current and frequented sources.

C. Make responsiveness a top priority.

As soon as you begin asking for help, recognize that you and the program will be judged by how effectively you respond to offers of help. So do not ask for help unless you are prepared to respond quickly to five, ten or twenty offers.

Questions and complaints should get top priority. Think of them like milk: left unattended, they can turn sour quickly. Create boilerplate answers that can be shared quickly and passed around by other managers when you are not available. It can become as basic as setting up a signature line in your email that has a link to your latest annual report or asks employees to tell you how you are doing, or to send you recommendations of employees to shine your CSR light on. You will find out quickly what the issues, questions, and opportunities are that keep popping up during your campaign, so as you go along, template as much as you can.

Once you have templated your information and your processes are in place, you will move easily from a start-up positioning to an internal consultant positioning. Your colleagues will see CSR as valued added because you are helping them engage and inspire their teams.

One benefit of the changing workplace behaviors brought on by social and mobile digital media is that it can be easier for your CSR program to attract attention as a kind of exciting internal "start-up" operation. It is human nature to be intrigued by new things, and as a start-up within the company, you are not bogged down by ingrained practices and expectations, the way existing departments are. Your newness gives you an initial window of opportunity to engage employees – much like an open window admitting fresh air. Do not squander this opportunity by failing to prepare for an enthusiastic employee response. Think through your one-two punch in advance.

For example, each time you convey a written message, such as an email or town-hall presentation, be sure to follow it up with a "trailer" – such as walking the halls and gathering employee feedback. You can also use a simple online survey service, like SurveyMonkey or Google Docs, to elicit quick specific and actionable ideas.

And if your CSR team is just you and another colleague, try to borrow some interns or junior staffers from other departments and enlist their support. You will be delighted to see how willing your colleagues are to volunteer a staffer for an hour or two and how inspired the junior staffers will be to get in on the ground floor of something so meaningful and filled with possibility. You will also be impressed with how plugged into your organization they are, and by the quality and quantity of unvarnished feedback they will get you.

A fun example of a one-two punch I have used involved LifeSavers Candies. As we developed employee volunteer fairs at Christie's London, New York and Hong Kong locations – what we called Arts Assemblies – we regularly communicated invitations and updates via online employee communications. To ensure a lasting and positive impression, we also followed up with each employee on the eve of the Arts Assemblies with individually wrapped LifeSaver Candies, to which we attached a brief rainbow colored message that said:

"Be a LifeSaver and visit the Arts Assembly
to see how you can make a difference
in a young person's life."

This approach had three noteworthy advantages. First, the Lifesaver candies for 2,000 employees cost less than $200, so they were a cheap and easy tool to use. Second, whenever employees were away from their desks, we were still able to drop our message in a way that broke through the clutter of their daily routines. Finally, sweets always sell. We had stellar turnouts at all of our Arts Assemblies, and never doubted that those LifeSaver reminders accounted for some degree of their success.

Arts Assembly Promotional Note that was Attached to Individually Wrapped LifeSaver Candies

BE A

LIFESAVER

DROP BY **THE ARTS ASSEMBLY** IN **18F VIEWING ROOMS 1, 2, AND 3** ON **AUGUST 7** FROM **10AM-12PM** TO MEET STAFF FROM MORE THAN 20 ARTS ORGANIZATIONS WHO WELCOME TALENTED VOLUNTEERS LIKE YOU.

As feedback flows into your CSR campaign, view each piece of feedback as an open loop in need of closure. To get this done quickly and efficiently, I recommend that you bucket all of the commentary you receive into well-defined topics or categories and prepare answers to each thematic area for your future campaign efforts. These can also be used with the FAQ previously discussed. Colleagues will know they have been heard and their opinions have been valued when you address them in this generic way through your actions. Remember to recognize employees by name when closing the feedback loop in public settings. Giving them a personal shout-out helps build your personal credibility and your program's credibility as a booster for workplace team spirit.

Another tool is to request or jump on any opportunities to address employee groups, from annual all-staff meetings to regional staff meetings to weekly team meetings. It will not take long after a few tries to arrive at a brief, standard talk that takes a matter of minutes, leaving time to engage them in richer one-on-one conversations. I always had a set of prepared questions to offer the audience, in case the audience was filled with members too shy to ask questions of their own.

In these talks, I always reminded my Christie's colleagues that I was there for them – that if an event or activity did not attract their involvement, then it was not worth doing. That perspective was valuable in inspiring volunteers to take ownership of various parts of our CSR. Then and to this day, whenever I talk about my colleagues' role in CSR, I tell them that my aim is to cast them as the heroes in our company's narrative. Not only does this have the benefit of being the truth, it is hard for most employees to demure from this casting.

The most valuable CSR feedback I have ever received has come from casual face-to-face encounters with my colleagues. For that reason, a key part of a CSR leader's job involves getting out from behind your desk. "You've got to walk the halls and really understand how they run the business," says Beth Colleton, formerly the chief sustainability officer at the NFL and NBCUniversal. "That's how you learn where their pressure points are and what they think their challenges are. Try to walk in their shoes. Remember, it's not what you're selling, it's what they're buying."

D. Nurture support from the top of the organization.

CSR gains so much of its strength from the top of the organization that the point cannot be repeated enough. When the CEO or company owner can see how CSR strategies are in direct in alignment with company initiatives toward cost reduction, revenue growth, and employee retention, that is when CSR really takes off.

It is up to you to nurture the connection between leadership and CSR, to make sure the company leadership sees this connection. Keep your top contacts in the company informed, involved and consulted. Pass along any communications showing that CSR has legitimate and broad-based support among employees.

The ideal CSR sponsor should always be your CEO or owner and you should make it as easy as possible for him or her to be engaged with CSR. If time constraints do not allow the CEO to attend a meeting in person, request a three or four-minute call-in on speaker phone. Offer to draft all-staff communications or annual report letters for their review and signature. Request them to make it a regular agenda item in their meetings with their direct reports, so it shows the CEO leading CSR by example. And as with your CEO or owner, be sure to make it as easy for executive-level direct reports to have the information and tools that they need to help you with the CSR campaign.

"We made CSR a CEO agenda item," says Rangu Salgame, former CEO of the Growth Ventures and Service Provider Group at Tata Communications. "It has to be for optimal success."

Bank of America Merrill Lynch in EMEA (Europe, Middle East, and Africa) has created an ESG governance structure where roles exist throughout the organization. "Our managing directors are sponsors of our ESG platform," says Andrea Sullivan. "Together with the ESG team, employees at all levels help roll out the initiatives and are encouraged and recognized for their efforts. This work also becomes a way to identify future leaders and build our culture."

To help hesitant executives engage with CSR, I made it a point to schedule in regular periods of 30-minutes or more to drop by an office or work station and engage senior (as well as more junior) employees about current affairs as well as CSR. For employees in other regions, I would substitute random phone calls to check in with colleagues. Believe it or not, no colleague ever told me that they did not have time to give me feedback about CSR. Your experience will likely be similar.

Too often executives can rationalize their being stuck at their desk by saying they are just too busy or by pointing to some erupting crisis. This isolation can be deadly for CSR efforts, but truth be told, the isolation can be more deadly for the longevity of the executive who does not regularly engage with rank and file employees. CSR can actually be a safe and easy way for them to engage with employees. Ironically, I have found that CSR is a way of giving executives permission to venture beyond their predicted routines and executive offices to engage employees in fresh and authentic ways.

Where this can get even more exciting is when your CEO makes it a point to regularly drop in to events where employees are engaged with customers and other stakeholders around a CSR activity. All three participants – the customer, the employee and the CEO – are affirmed by such an interaction. JPMorgan Chase CEO Jamie Dimon is a rock star in this practice. He regularly shows up for what I call "drive-by's" which are seemingly impromptu 5-minute visits with informal but strategically important remarks.

Dimon did this on one occasion with an organization I was on the board of – the Empire State Pride Agenda, an LGBTQ advocacy group in New York State. Each year we hosted a "Pride in the Workplace" luncheon that recognized companies who were fostering more diverse and inclusive workplaces in New York. One year, JPMorgan Chase provided their elegant boardroom and catering facilities to host the awards luncheon for 150 LGBTQ leaders, hosted by the bank's dynamic Chief Communications Officer Joe Evangelisti. Imagine the room's shock and delight when

Jamie not only dropped by but gave Joe a huge bear hug and then in fewer than five minutes impressed upon the group how important a core value diversity and inclusion is at JPMorgan Chase. Google "CSR" and "JPMorgan Chase" and you will begin to see what best-in-class CSR looks like at one the largest, most heavily regulated banks in the world. From the top down, the bank strives to raise its level of play every day. As recently as June 2018, when the US government was separating migrant families at the border, Dimon wrote to his employees outlining his opposition to the policy, citing American values as well as making the case that fixing the nation's immigration problems "will clearly boost the economy and help companies like ours hire great talent."

"You have to be sure that the top management is really involved in this journey," says Marie-Claire Daveu, chief sustainability officer and head of international institutional affairs at Paris-based Kering. "Without the top management really convinced and really involved nothing will happen. It is not just a question of money. Most important for me is change management. To push people to go beyond classical boundaries, you need to have this kind of involvement, involvement with a vision; it's about making it clear to people that sustainability is not an option but a business and long-term necessity."

In retrospect, I could have and should have done much more at Christie's to engage the three CEO's I worked under through the years in our CSR efforts. I probably let them off the hook too easily for fear of rejection. The truth is that it is very easy to not do these things. I never challenged my CEO to help me find a better way to get more participation and cooperation from senior management. For instance, I settled for having a small, representative group of executives at my group presentations, and many of them frequently bowed out because of pressing deadlines and priorities. If I had been more honest with myself in the early days, I would have acknowledged to myself and then my CEO that senior management needed to be more present at these meetings. When company leadership is missing, it is too easy for CSR to take on the aura of a "nice to have" exercise, and not the mission-critical, brand-building, employee-morale boosting enterprise that it can be.

2.2. Strategy execution

In Chapter One, your research within your company revealed where the company is already doing the right thing. Now, as you develop a holistic CSR program, you can begin to define strategies for maximizing those efforts. As you inventory your company's ongoing socially responsible activities in various departments, look for examples where quick modifications, reframing or simple publicity could help demonstrate the possibilities of your longer-term CSR strategies. Places to start might include the company recycling program, Energy Saver appliance usage or a lights-off-when-not-working policy. My previous example of simply tracking auctioneering that benefits not-for-profit organizations is again an example of this. We were doing it all along, but we never really took credit for it or talked about it.

Supporting existing activities

As you grow you can recognize employee volunteer practices already in place, such showcasing employee fundraisers such as cancer walks or Corporate Challenges. Here again, JPMorgan Chase provides a great example. Globally, thousands of companies participate in the JPMorgan Corporate Challenge races for charity each year. The participating companies sponsor tens of thousands of employees in the races. There is nothing like a group photo of victorious racers on your company intranet to show true team spirit and a collective effort to make the world a better place. And it is shareable once it is online, only amplifying your message more.

Try to support movements that are unique to your company's location and its particular challenges. Be sensitive to the pressing problems on everyone's mind, and where their organizations in need of help. In Hong Kong, for instance, where there is a stark disparity between the haves and have-nots, the organization Helping Hands Hong Kong provides your company with the chance to create mentor opportunities for underprivileged young people. This is one of the partners we chose to work with in tailoring our volunteerism to local needs at Christie's.

This is the opportunity to explore where your company's volunteerism of in-kind industry-specific goods and services could step up. At Christie's, I have discussed the sales in which the auction proceeds are directed to a charity of the client's choice. And the numbers are impressive each year. But beyond auctions on behalf of clients, Christie's also provides auctioneers for not-for-profit organizations' fundraising galas, going above and beyond the auction house's traditional salesroom and sales calendar to help charitable organizations and causes.

Prior to the launch of Art + Soul, these activities of our charity auctioneers had never been tracked and reported on internally. Christie's trained charity auctioneers conduct countless auctioneers globally on behalf of charities as diverse as Helen Keller International, the Jewish Aging Services Administration, Doctors Without Borders, Oceana, and Nelson Mandela Foundation. By formally counting the number of auctions conducted and dollars raised for these and other worthy causes, we captured unique and inspiring stories to tell our employees and outside stakeholders. It was easy to do and gave us an opportunity to shine a light on our colleagues and make them feel appreciated.

Start small and allow colleagues to pick up your tune

Big companies have the opportunity to make big impact with CSR, but smaller companies, especially private companies still managed by their founders, also have a great chance of having CSR make a big impact on them. With close-knit cultures and just one or two worksites, small companies have an advantage to create fast change that can make an immediate impact on the company's bottom-line, and its reputation.

Regardless of the size or nature of your company, assume a campaign position, work the troops that you have, and do not lose sight of your end goal, which a sustainable business that profits while making its communities stronger. To paraphrase a one-time U.S. defense secretary, you go to war with the army you have, which is not necessarily the one you want or wish you had.

Our CSR army at Christie's was a bit ragtag. It was officially me, one coordinator and two college interns. But we tapped into a legion of colleagues who we had identified with our listening tour and whose roles in the business dovetailed with our CSR program. For example, Toby Monk ran recruiting for our Human Resources department in London and was beautifully positioned to help us roll out and manage our volunteer activities there. Karen Gray, our General Counsel in New York, was a strong advocate for all of our efforts, and showed up for all of our events, and leveraged her team and resources to help our campaign. In London, Giles Mountain from our Facilities team was our reporting guru when it came to tracking Christie's use of water, electricity, and waste management services. We had to divide to conquer, and we did, with the ragtag army that we had.

Even at big companies, single worksites are capable of beginning small CSR effort that can catch fire throughout the organization. Back in 1983, the cast members at Disneyland Resort expressed a desire to form a community service group that would do work to benefit non-profit organizations in Orange County, California. This sincere desire took form as the Disneyland Community Action Team, which was at first a fairly modest initiative. However, the work of the team earned so much notoriety for Disney and its charitable partners that by 1992 it had had inspired the company-wide launch of Disney VoluntEARS.

Today, Disney VoluntEARS work on meaningful projects across the globe, primarily on benefiting children and families in communities where Disney business units operate. In 2015 Disney VoluntEARS provided more than 83,000 hours of their time at 235 local events. Organizations nominated by cast members received more than $350,000 in grants through an employee-managed community fund. Another program, called EARS to You, allows cast member to turn their volunteer hours into financial contributions to non-profits of their choosing, generating more than $200,000 to organizations in Disney communities.

Disney VoluntEARS gives Disney a chance to be a good neighbor in its communities, promote the company culture as a caring one, and give its employees unique opportunities for community service. It is a great example of how CSR activities can align company culture-building, talent retention, and brand promotion.

Put your money where your mouth is

VoluntEARS would not have taken off as an idea if Disney had not been willing to devote some resources toward its success. Many companies are discovering that community service volunteer work is so important to their brand image and employee happiness that they are sponsoring "volunteer" events while employees are still on the clock. An estimated 20% of employers now provide workers with a bank of paid time off that is set aside specifically for volunteering – up from about 15% in 2009.

In Minneapolis, where U.S. Bank is headquartered, a group of U.S. Bank employees skips the office on Friday mornings and works at a local soup kitchen instead. Employees are given several days per year where they can, in essence, take extra paid vacation time to support the company's community service efforts. In 2017, their employees donated 188,000 hours of volunteer time, which the bank valued at $4.5 million in support to the communities in which it operates.

For your company, this might mean paying your employees during their volunteer time out of the office, funding community efforts around megatrends (e.g., climate, education, healthcare), or giving enough budget to your CSR program to have greater impact.

Activities of this kind have been common in legal services and other professions, where employers are expected to support the tradition of employees devoting a certain percentage of their time to pro bono work. Extending the pro bono concept to other workplaces, however, is in response to the very real problem of retaining good employees. Offering employees the opportunity to bond with each other while doing good also helps the company's culture and employee morale – an important consideration when you consider the previously cited Korn Ferry finding that only 36% of organizational talent feels highly engaged with their work.

To the extent your company is able to support it and deliver it correctly, one of the major advantages of CSR work is that it is meaningful and rewarding. Paying employees to do a few days' work per year for volunteer time out of the office may prove to be of the best Human Resources investments your company can make.

2.3. The power of networking with CSR colleagues

When I began with CSR, I felt very much on my own at first. CSR was still too new as a discipline to have any established professional groups for me to engage with. Today I see CSR training programs and membership organizations popping up regularly, and there may be some value in participating them in order to get a view of the field and build a network for yourself.

Personally, I generally avoid these groups because my own network is already fairly robust and none of the existing groups address my particular business needs. The added obstacle is that conferences and associations require investments of time and money – and I have always found better things to do with those resources. Marie-Claire Daveu, Kering's chief sustainability officer and head of international institutional affairs, says that it can be more strategic to attend trade conventions and conferences within your industry, and then seek out sessions on sustainability issues there. "We are approached often for speaking engagements," she says. "It's sometimes even more interesting when the conference is not strictly on sustainability, but on business, luxury or fashion and then they want to include a sustainability angle." However, she notes that sustainability conferences that attract a lot of influential activist and non-governmental organizations can also be very important to attend.

The one big exception I made to my rule of avoiding CSR programs turned out to be one of the best things I ever did. I enrolled at a 3-day executive education program on sustainability at Harvard Business School. That is where I "got religion" about CSR, thanks to the tutelage of Professors Robert Eccles and George Serafeim, leading researchers in proving that sustainability makes good business sense. It was at this event that my network of top CSR professionals grew by about 40, including people from leading firms such as Hess and Nutrea.

Building such a network is invaluable for testing ideas, borrowing ideas that work and sharing what has worked for you. It is also valuable for emotional support, because leading CSR can be lonely. Ask around to see what programs or membership organizations are most important to CSR practitioners in your industry or region. You could learn a lot, save some time, and also make some lasting friendships.

The professional listening tour

At the same time that I was doing my internal listening tour at Christie's, I also undertook an informal professional listening tour among other CSR practitioners, including those I met at Harvard Business School. Beyond HBS alumni, I focused my tour on CSR in multinational corporations that have worksites on several continents, because geography and time zones were significant challenges facing me at Christie's.

I spent time on the phone and in meetings and on business trips consulting with heads of CSR at Hershey, PepsiCo, American Express, BNY Mellon, Bank of America Merrill Lynch, Proskauer, Korn Ferry, and Goldman Sachs, just to name a few. I quickly learned how the CSR community is just that – a community of individuals with a shared sense of purpose in making the world a better place. We are all in this together so we help each other however we can.

Through my 25 years of experience in corporate communications, I had a ready-made network of leaders in that field who could make introductions for my professional CSR listening tour. You may not enjoy the same specific advantage, but you should try to use whatever existing network you already have to reach out the CSR programs at other companies. For instance, if you have ever worked with an executive recruiter or professional services provider (such as an auditor or lawyer) that serves peer companies, check in to let them know about your initiative and ask them if they can introduce you to kindred spirits. Remember that they are professional connectors, and most of them enjoy making new mutually beneficial introductions.

Secondly, you will find new contacts by checking the CSR reports of peer companies, vendors or perhaps companies adjacent to yours in a larger company's supply chain. The existing relationship between your companies gives you the opening to discuss their reports and once engaged, ask them for advice on your work. The research and reading that you do will also be beneficial to the shaping of your own program.

A third approach is to follow online CSR networks such as those on LinkedIn, and then engage those whose insight or opinions resonate with you. You will likely be delighted at how professional and responsive your CSR peers are. That is one of the great attributes of the practice area – people care about creating positive and lasting ripple effects, of which you are a part.

In general, you want to reach out to people in companies you would consider peers of yours, but it is also worthwhile to seek out CSR professionals who arrived at CSR through the same route as you, whether it is through Corporate Communications, Legal, Human Resources, or Operations. With that shared background and shared perspective of organizational dynamics, you will find plenty to talk about, even if your companies are very different.

Judy Tenzer who helped launch and manage American Express's CSR efforts, was my first port of call since we had worked together there in the 1990s. She suggested digging into your digital network, starting with LinkedIn but extending into other social media platforms (e.g., Facebook, WhatsApp, WeChat, Snapchat) to jog your memory on who you can consult.

As cited previously with JPMorgan Chase, leverage the digital technology and search your network for such key words as "CSR" and "Sustainability" and "Corporate Citizenship" to see who else you may have missed. Do an online search of brands that inspire you, and simply adding words like "CSR" or "sustainability" in the search bar will yield a bounty of potential contacts to reach out to for your listening tour. Via LinkedIn, you can reach out to them directly or simply ask the organizers to give you a selection of alumni or member names to contact. It cannot hurt, and it will also grow your CSR network without spending a dime.

Start your own CSR association

When I began to run the Corporate Communications team at Christie's in the early 2000s, my peers in the art ecosystem were few and far between. I would go to corporate communications events and find myself somewhat lonely, with little to contribute. I realized that although Christie's is a for-profit company, it is also an arts organization, and I had much more in common with communications professionals in the arts.

So I set out to create ArtsCom, an invitation-only membership organization made up of the chief communications officers from all of the top-flight cultural institutions in greater New York, including the Metropolitan Museum, MoMA, Carnegie Hall, Brooklyn Museum, New York Public Library, and others. Now 10 years old, the communicators get together once a month, and in lieu of membership dues, members are asked to host a quarterly breakfast once every two years. The project was so rewarding that in 2011, my co-founder Mary Trudell and I built a second chapter of ArtsCom in London with another friend Julian Bird, former chief operating officer of the Tate Group of museums and now CEO of the Society of London Theater Owners (SOLT).

Together we shared networks, information, insights, support, and goodwill. Within our respective organizations, we discovered that we were all the "odd ducks" who had much more in common with each other than with our everyday work colleagues. The same is true of CSR professionals. No one else has a role in the workplace quite like it, and there is likely no one in your workplace that can really understand the challenges you face.

Starting your own "odd duck" group locally, by bringing together all the nearby CSR professionals, might be one of the most valuable things you can do for your CSR effort. On the odd chance that there is already such a local organization up and running, consider joining. Quarterly meetings of this kind can help remind you that there is always more to know, and the plenty of others have gone before you and will be happy to help you in your new role. That is part of the power of CSR. It always gets stronger through inclusion and collaboration.

There is a beautiful circular nature to building a CSR platform with a legion of supporters. The more you campaign, the more capacity you build, the better your CSR program and its network becomes. For me, it could have been a lonely place, having gone from nearly a decade of running a 30-person global communications team to launching a 2-full-time-staff CSR department. But I saw the challenge as an opportunity, primarily because I believed in the mission. Rather than feeling alone, I sought out advice and inspiration from outside my company among those had pioneered CSR in their own companies. Then I layered in the wealth of knowledge and networks available through professional associations such as IABC, SASB, and others, as noted previously. And then, as the ultimate expression of arrival, I created new organizations – particularly ArtsCom New York and ArtsCom London – which not only addressed my professional networking needs, but also advanced the CSR mission of Christie's and filled a void in our sector.

CHAPTER THREE
Convene and Connect

"When you were made a leader you weren't given a crown,
you were given the responsibility to bring out the best in others."
– Jack Welch

In 2005 General Electric introduced a new initiative called Ecomagination, an ambitious, groundbreaking strategy that would redefine what it meant for a company of GE's size to "go green." Through partnerships with companies such as Wal-Mart and Intel, GE developed renewable energy projects in emerging markets, high-efficiency commercial lighting, and manufacturing techniques that cut energy costs and reduce water waste.

For decades, GE had ranked among the world's most admired companies and best places to work. But only after the launch of Ecomagination did it earn distinctions for social responsibility. The company also took a leadership role as corporate citizen. GE's Supplier Expectations[10] govern all facets of its with suppliers, with specific prohibitions against human trafficked, forced labor, prison labor, and indentured labor. During Volunteers Global Month of Service, GE coordinates efforts to address urgently needed engineering projects around the world.

Ecomagination projects generated more than $200 billion in revenues since its 2005 launch. It became a leading strategy in GE's transformation from a sprawling conglomerate to a new identity as a "digital industrial" company. Since the launch of Ecomagination, GE sold off most of its interests in real estate, banking, insurance, financial services, media, and entertainment. At the same time, the company increased investments in wind power and energy-efficient lighting.

However, in 2017, GE suffered from a tremendous reversal of fortunes. In recent years, the GE Power division, one of GE's largest, had made sizable investments in turbines and generators used by coal and natural gas power plants. Construction of these plants soon went into sharp decline, thanks to competition from renewable wind and solar power sources. In retrospect, GE did not take

Ecomagination idea far enough. As GE Stock prices tumbled by 40% in 2017, the company went into turnaround mode. GE has sought to expand its renewable power division with a $1.6 billion purchase of a Danish maker of wind rotor blades, even as GE continues to shed other, less-profitable divisions.

On GE's web portal for CSR, there is this simple, succinct statement: "GE's business is fundamentally about people: our employees, our customers, our investors and the members of the communities where we live and operate."[11] That lineup of stakeholders, one shared by most companies with a strong CSR focus, could be depicted as a target with concentric rings. At the center of the target, the bullseye, are GE employees. Outside the bullseye is the inner ring for GE customers and investors. The outer ring is the broader community in which GE operates – its industries, employee locations, and markets, which encircle the globe.

Beginning at the bullseye and moving outward, it is useful think of your CSR targets in a similar way – your people, your customers, and your planet. You want to start aiming your company's CSR arrows in all three areas, because success in one area can be a force-multiplier in the other areas. A motivated workforce active in CSR is better prepared to engage and support the customer-facing CSR marketing with enthusiasm and integrity. Sustainable products and business practices further motivate employees. And when the company's CEO and other executives take leadership roles in CSR within their communities and industries, it inspires faith in the company among customers and all the company's stakeholders. The CSR target is an integrated model, and working at all three target areas has the potential to change and uplift the company's entire culture.

Bullseye of Audiences for your CSR and General Business Efforts

3.1. Employees – The Bullseye

Company-led CSR activities are becoming an employee expectation, according to some surveys. Particularly among younger employees, there is a belief that CSR is something the employer should provide, no different than any other item in their benefits package. Company-wide days of service and other CSR activities are growing in importance because they help busy employees fulfill their needs for giving back and feeling connected with co-workers.

This development provides enlightened employers with tremendous opportunities, if they are willing to establish CSR within the company culture. Employees bond over their shared interest in greater causes. CSR gives them a chance to develop cross-departmental relationships that take the corporate hierarchy out of the picture. It is good for team building, fostering a shared sense of purpose and overall morale. At its best, CSR makes a difference, and in doing so, makes employees feel better about themselves, their colleagues and their employer.

Volunteer and charity events are the bread-and-butter for CSR engagement with your employees. Whether they are volunteer days or outdoor charity fundraisers, most successful CSR event share these four essential features:

- Low barriers to participation in terms of time, cost, and preparation.
- Large social component, such as a picnic or party at the end of charity walk.
- Souvenirs in the form of t-shirts, medals, or team photos.
- Visible participation by senior executives.

As you aim to convene and connect, there is no shortage of opportunities for participating in existing CSR events. As noted previously, the JPMorgan Chase Corporate Challenge, an annual fundraising 5K race in major cities around the world, is just one example of an excellent turnkey program that any size company can tap into.

Ideas for these events, wherever they come from, work best when they have been tested on online workplace forums. It is particularly smart to solicit feedback from those within the workplace who know your brand the best.

When recruiting participants in any CSR activity, you might want to try seeing it as an opportunity to expand your CSR community beyond the limits of the current payroll. Consider your company's alumni, current technology partners, suppliers, major customers, the offices of elected officials, and other friends of your company. At Christie's we engaged hundreds of alumni in our CSR efforts with Art + Soul, and it benefited the company because we were able to develop an alumni network on LinkedIn at no cost. We even included the New York City Cultural Commissioner and a City Councilmember along the way. I simply followed the model of another venerable institution – Goldman Sachs – in using LinkedIn as our means to an end.

Social media is an ideal way to reach out to establish these ties to the organization, with CSR as the rallying point. In the case of our alumni, we were careful not to bombard them with constant messages, so they were generally grateful to hear about the good things Art + Soul was doing when we shared that information with them.

In everything you do, using social media platforms from Facebook to Instagram to WeChat is essential to your success with CSR campaigns. As numbers of Millennials and younger digital natives increasingly predominate in the workplace, directing your communications through their favored modes of contact becomes ever more important.

In China, hundreds of employees of the Esquel Company volunteer each year in health programs in the country's rural areas. Through social media "not only have they communicated their positive feedback, they are also more motivated to make donations and devote their time to volunteering," says John Cheh, Vice Chairman and CEO of Esquel. After a social media campaign promoting an eye health program in rural Xinjiang, he adds, "we have seen` an increased number of staff volunteering for the program and organizing donations for eyeglasses."

The key to engaging workers in CSR is emphasizing the community aspect of the process. Employees want to feel like they are working together for the greater good and that they have a voice in the process.

Along those lines, "micro-volunteering" is a trending phenomenon which uses apps and web platforms to offers workplace volunteers ways of taking action on CSR causes in short bursts of activity. This is not for everyone, and certainly lacks a social component, but for remote workers and hardworking younger employees, it might hold a certain appeal.

Possibilities range from online petition-signing to crowdsourced proofreading of literature in translation. Companies like Skills for Change offer businesses platforms – a sort of turnkey solution to get your employees together one or another group endeavor. The Nielsen Company, with employees all over the world, addressed the challenge of coordinating their annual "Global Impact Day" by partnering with YourCause.com. One large benefit of such programs is that they are able to track participation levels and establish baseline numbers from which to grow.

At Christie's, we worked for a time with a similar service called VolunteerMatch. Although we had some success with it, we eventually concluded that it was adding an unnecessary layer of organization between our employees and our impact. For us, we found we could tee up our own set of pre-arranged volunteer opportunities, which were fewer in number but larger and more meaningful in ultimate impact. For many companies, VolunteerMatch is an excellent way to get up and running fast. You may stick with it in the long-term, or, like Christie's, you might cast it off like a set of training wheels.

The consultant WeSpire's 2015 employee survey, "The Evolution of Employee Engagement," looked at the direct and indirect factors impacting employee engagement across organizations including the role of the manager, corporate transparency, and employee choice and collaboration.[12] The report reveals that only 27% of organizations have an official employee engagement policy, and further, 76% of employees under the age of 30 (younger members of the Millennial generation) want to see their employer do more around employee engagement.

It is clear that it is time for a sea change in the way corporate social responsibility is structured. According to consulting giant PWC, a whopping 90% of recent graduates – the leading edge of a post-Millennial generation, the so-called Generation Z – say they seek employers whose social responsibility priorities reflect their own.[13] These younger workers, with a world of information at their fingertips and an affinity for sharing online, expect transparency about where their time and dollars are donated. Real-time we are watching the Gen Z response to the Parkland, Florida, school shootings and it is formidable. In addition to giving the students a platform and campaign, it has captured major support from businesses such as Delta, United, Hertz, and several insurers. Some human resources departments have grown accustomed making decisions of this kind behind closed doors, perhaps under the assumption that no one cared as long as the cause was a good one. Those days are coming to an end.

Your default positioning should be oriented toward the concept of community – fostering it, investing in it and celebrating it. The reason is that it makes sense to the bottom line, and there is a growing risk in not being part of it, as the businesses responding to Parkland's #NeverAgain movement are finding.

Employee engagement initiatives are more important than ever, along with CSR and sustainability in the business world. These areas will not only continue to differentiate the leaders from the followers, they will likely be the key to survival. This gives the concept of sustainability even broader and more meaningful definition. The PWC report goes on to predict a "people management model for the Green World" in which CSR and human resources are fused, and "the people management function is forced to embrace sustainability as part of its people engagement and talent management agendas."

For management it is good for operations, efficiency, the bottom line, and professional development. Creating a platform that unites customers, employees and community members around a higher purpose is good business. It also helps break down silos, identifies rising talent, allows for growth opportunities when budgets and promotions are tight, and reflects well on a brand.

To build solid foundations for their CSR efforts, many companies are linking purposeful activities to their own core competencies, allowing them to highlight the impact they are making on society while showcasing the value of their expertise in the real world.

For example, Microsoft's CSR underscores technology as a powerful force for improving people's lives. Since approximately half of the world does not have access to the benefits and opportunities that technology offers, the company's 114,000 employees are committed to doing more globally to bring the benefits of technology to the people and organizations who need them most. Together with Microsoft grantees, partners, and employees globally, they aim "to empower every person and every organization on the planet to achieve more." As a result, for decades Microsoft has ranked among the top places to work.

In a similar vein, global manufacturer 3M partnered with Discovery Education to create the Young Scientist Challenge, a mentorship program that identifies talented young minds and gives them the opportunity to work with professional scientists to brainstorm innovative, real-world solutions to significant societal challenges.

This advanced type of CSR puts its focus on developing new employees, recruiting, and planning for future hiring. It builds from the core strength of the company, and in addition to contributing financially, it leverages in-kind resources that include talent, facilities, knowledge, networks. Ultimately it aims for a higher, noble purpose, and does so in a declarative and transparent manner. Promotion, internal and external, are important in raising the company's reputation and achieving the desired uplifting effect among employees and other stakeholders.

3.2. Customers – The Middle Ring of the Bullseye

Customers are not that different than employees. They like companies that make them feel good about associating with them. Customers want to spend money in a socially responsible way, and when your company's communications are effective in delivering a CSR message about what you sell, the resulting emotional connection with customers tends to engender brand loyalty.

For all these reasons and many others, there are vast opportunities in CSR marketing. As brands evolve with the times, CSR can build lasting relationships between consumers and brands because the engagement involves consumer convictions and beliefs, not just transactional purchasing.

Selling through CSR is somewhat like moving customers upwards through Maslow's hierarchy of needs. Customers of all ages are looking to define their purpose and place in communities and the world. They seek relationships with brands that are doing the same within their own value set. As a result, every business needs to ask itself, "What is the impact of our activities on each other, the community, the workplace, customers, and the planet?" Companies that can provide satisfactory answers to this question have a leg up on the competition for CSR-driven dollars, euros, and yuan.

Coldwell Banker offers a simple example of how CSR has emerged as a marketing tool.[14] In 2017, the company ran an ad campaign that promoted its Homes for Dogs Project, a partnership with Adopt-a-Pet.com that has helped find homes for more than 20,000 dogs "because everyone deserves a loving home." In years past, the company might have run a similarly heartwarming ad about a stray dog finding a new home, but without the company engaging the issue and making an actual difference for homeless dogs. Today's customers have wised up to those kinds of empty advertising images. They want to know how you are achieving positive results.

SurveyMonkey, the online survey provider, has created a separate service called Audience, as a way to extend its expertise to deserving causes across the country. Instead of offering cash and prizes to survey takers (its normal business model) SurveyMonkey uses Audience to donate 50 cents for each completed survey to the survey taker's charity of choice. In 2013 alone, the company donated more than $1 million to organizations such as the Humane Society, Boys & Girls Club of America, and Teach for America.[15] In this case, the CSR "give back" really communicates and asserts SurveyMonkey's belief in CSR while also underscoring its survey capabilities – a win-win for the company and the causes it supports.

For companies that sell business-to-business (B2B) products, CSR provides marketers a chance to make their customers the heroes of their sustainability stories. SAP Ariba is the world's largest business-to-business network, connecting more than 3.4 million buyers and sellers in 190 countries. The company, has a Procure with Purpose program that helps businesses around the world identify risks in their supply chains, ranging from unfair labor conditions to unsustainable environmental factors. SAP Ariba promises, "With this level of clarity, you can improve the societal, economic, and environmental impact of your business and every organization and community it touches."

"Our customers are people in unsung positions such as the head of finance or supply chain management," says Jennifer Beason, head of communications, SAP Corporate Social Responsibility. "Now we're giving them the tools and strategic guidance to make a big difference on these issues. We bring them up on the big stage at our conferences. They tell these heart-wrenching stories about their leadership and their courage in being a pioneer in ethical sourcing." In one of SAP Ariba's marketing materials, a procurement officer at a client company is quoted as saying, "When my kids ask me 'what did you do today?' I don't want to tell them that I saved a bunch of money. I want to tell them I saved lives."

Marketing-oriented CSR has some serious its pitfalls, including clumsy messaging, product gimmickry, and a poor fit between the company image and the cause involved. The greatest hazard is getting a reputation for "greenwashing" – which is similar to whitewashing as a method of covering up embarrassing truths, but using environmental claims to do it.

The term "greenwashing" was coined in the 1980s when Chevron proudly promoted its environmental programs, many of which were simply mandated by law. The company also used a lavish ad campaign to trumpet its support of a butterfly preserve, when an environmentalist noted that while the butterfly preserve cost Chevron about $5,000 per year, the ads promoting it cost millions to produce and broadcast. Around the same time, chemical company DuPont was running ads featuring marine animals clapping their flippers to Beethoven's Ode to Joy while a report on the company called "Hold the Applause" showed DuPont was the single largest corporate polluter in the U.S.[16]

In the 1980s, a report like "Hold the Applause" was difficult to distribute, and no match for DuPont's reach in terms of advertising dollars. Today the facts in a report of that kind would be re-tweeted all over the world in seconds. The world is no longer a safe place for corporate greenwashing. If you pretend to care about a cause you align with, or a cause that is important to your customer, all you will do is strike a false note that could open your company to ridicule and devastate the company's reputation.

Authenticity and caring to make a difference need to be part of your company culture. It is best if those same qualities can also be found in the products and services you sell. CSR-oriented marketing is at its most persuasive when it is executed around products or services that have inherent, essential components of CSR.

Starbucks, for example, was the first major coffee maker to advance the concept of sourcing "free-trade" coffee beans that are ethically purchased and responsibly produced. Efforts of this kind succeed when they educate the consumer and inspire product loyalty, but in a humble way that is not snobbish, patronizing or condescending. The types of consumers that will pay a little extra for sustainable products and materials tend to be turned off by bragging or claims of being special. If you happen to be the maker of the only sustainably sourced product in your industry or category, it is not an appropriate occasion for boasting. The responsible thing to do is to join with your competitors and persuade them that your whole sector would do better if it were a maker of sustainable products.

More recently, Starbucks has repeated this approach of collaboration by joining a coalition of businesses and not-for-profit organizations in moving away from the use of plastic straws by 2020.[17] As CEO Kevin Johnson noted that the decision came in response to requests from employees and customers alike. The ripple effect is a potential tidal wave against plastic pollution, eliminating more than a billion straws served at its stores annually.

Helping set new standards for behavior within your industry can produce transformative results. That is the intent behind luxury group Kering's decision in 2018 to publish the Kering Standards, a set of environmental and social standards for manufacturing processes and raw materials in the fashion industry. Having found there were no existing standards and regulations for its industry, Kering worked with experts and non-profit organizations to define a set of desirable sustainability standards of its own, with the hope that other industry members would also adopt them.

"We are redesigning our business to continue to thrive and prosper sustainably into the future," says Kering CEO François-Henri Pinault, "while at the same time helping to transform the luxury sector and contributing to meet the significant social and environmental challenges of our generation."

Kering has opened a Materials Innovation Lab, located in Novara, Italy, which has sourced sustainable wool from Patagonia and is working with a start-up called Worn Again to develop methods of recycling polyester. The lab maintains a comprehensive library of more than 3,000 certified fabrics which are ranked for sustainability against external standards, as well as the lab's own sustainability evaluation tool.

"At Kering, our goal is to reduce our environmental footprint by 40% across the entire supply chain by 2025 and innovation is key to achieve this," says Marie-Claire Daveu, Kering's chief sustainability officer and head of international institutional affairs. "We feel because we are in luxury and because luxury sets the trends, we have a specific responsibility to help show the way, to be an example, and to be sure in these new trends that sustainability is really included."

That is the ethos that socially conscious consumers want from the people they spend money with. Customers of sustainable businesses want them to be profitable. They want to be reassured that in the long run sustainable is smart and makes good business sense.

Business leaders are noticing that today's affluent consumers do not always like the choices they have been given. "People are walking out of brands that they've been consuming for decades," Emmanuel Faber, CEO of Danone, told the Economist in 2018. Danone has launched a new vision statement titled "Danone: One Planet, One Health" which calls for new sustainable models of food production that emphasize local sourcing. "We believe a healthy body needs healthy food," the statement declares. "And healthy food needs a healthy planet."[18]

In recent years, there have been a large number of startup companies that originate with CSR as a major product feature. These purpose-driven companies have invented the concept of philanthropic branding. The founder of Toms shoes was inspired to start the company while traveling in Peru and seeing barefoot children whose families could not afford shoes for them. The marketing thrust of Toms shoes is that for every pair bought by a consumer, another pair would be given through a charity in Peru. Toms Shoes, an example that is known to most as one of the pioneers in CSR, went from $9 million to $21 million in revenue in just three years by being a "purpose-driven brand" that enables people to give back to others simply by making a purchase. This concept of buy-one-give-one has spawned countless imitators, tying marketing of the product directly to sales and consumer choice.

Imported products are developed and marketed now as economic development projects in African, Asian and Latin American countries. The cosmetics company Out of Africa does more than just purchase high-quality shea-butter skin care products. It also helps improve the quality of life for West African women and children. A portion of Out of Africa's proceeds is donated to organizations that provide education and medical care to children, and the company regularly donates to women's cooperatives that create jobs in West Africa.

Purpose-driven companies have been around a long time. For more than 25 years, Seventh Generation has been formulating plant-based household products that are safe and that work. As such, any connecting with the brand is arguably "nurturing the health of the next seven generations." Seventh Generation employees believe their products are healthy solutions for the air, surfaces, fabrics, pets, and people within a customer's home – and for the community and environment outside of it. A pioneer in corporate responsibility, Seventh Generation wanted their products to make a difference – from their development through to their production, purchase, use, and disposal. To this day, the company continually evaluates how to reduce their environmental impact, increase performance and safety, and create a more sustainable supply chain.

In certain smaller start-ups like Etsy, whose existence derives from an online community with intense shared interests and values, transformative CSR is nearly invisible. To the consumer's eye, CSR is almost indistinguishable from the business itself. Wherever a company is placed on this "visibility spectrum" for CSR, the best companies share certain common characteristics: 1) authenticity in their CSR mission and initiatives, 2) ongoing dialogue with their customers and larger community around their CSR, and 3) a commitment to ongoing innovation and experimentation in pursuit of the CSR mission.

All three points are certainly true of Seventh Generation. Although the company has just a fraction of the sales of its huge consumer-product competitors, it was nonetheless purchased by Unilever in 2016 for an estimated $700 million – nearly three times its annual sales revenues. It is one of many cases in which huge consumer product conglomerates have purchased purpose-driven brands, rather than attempt to compete with them. Usually, the acquired brands downplay their parent company relationships. They operate as independent, wholly-owned subsidiaries, in order to maintain their magic bond with customers.

Method is a Seventh Generation competitor and another example of a purpose-driven household product manufacturer with strict standards for sustainability. The company has been purchased twice in recent years. First it was bought by the European giant Ecover in 2012. Then both Method and Ecover were purchased in 2017 by U.S.-based SC Johnson. However, on the SC Johnson website, Method and Ecover are nowhere to be seen among the SC Johnson "family" of traditional brands such as Windex, Drano, and Raid insect spray.

Unilever's plan with Seventh Generation is similar, to leave it as a standalone unit, and allow the parent and subsidiary to learn from each other. That was Unilever's approach to another socially responsible company it purchased: Ben & Jerry's Ice Cream. After the Unilever takeover in 2000, Ben & Jerry's continued its practice of employee-led corporate philanthropy and making generous product donations to community groups for fundraisers and the like. When Unilever instituted its tried-and-true goal-oriented performance management system at the company, Ben & Jerry's managers responded by adding a new dimension to Unilever's system – performance measures for maintaining the company's social mission.

In that way and others, both the parent and subsidiary can grow and improve. As long as sustainable companies such as Seventh Generation, Ben and Jerry's, and Method continue to deliver the three critical customer-facing elements of authenticity, dialogue, and CSR innovation, their parent company ownership will remain more or less invisible to the customers that love them.

3.3 The Outer Ring of the Bullseye: Community and the World

When companies engage with their larger communities through philanthropic associations and other kinds of coalitions, they send the strongest possible signal to their employees and customers that the commitment to CSR comes right from the top. Participation in local, industry-wide, national, and international CSR efforts enhances the company's reputation among customers and infuses employees with a greater sense of meaning for their work, because their company is truly dedicated to making a difference.

"We believe it is important to regularly review our stakeholder identification process," says John Cheh, Vice Chairman and CEO of at Esquel Group, the textile manufacturer. "It is about building relationships that share common values and creating synergy." Esquel's broad list of stakeholders include the Fair Labor Association, Sustainable Apparel Coalition, and all the suppliers, communities, and regulatory agencies that they are involved with.

One easy way for any company to engage with the larger community in CSR is through existing coalitions and organizations established to address specific concerns, such as poverty, veterans' affairs, or financial literacy.

If you are just starting your CSR efforts or you need to take small steps and build support over time, consider joining a coalition such as these. Linking arms with others who share your CSR interests is efficient, effective, and plugs you into a much larger network of creative, solutions-oriented peers. To illustrate, here are just three examples of such organizations I have had personal experiences with:

- The Robin Hood Foundation combines investment principles with philanthropy to assist anti-poverty programs that target poverty in New York City. It was founded in 1988 by hedge fund manager Paul Tudor Jones, and its board of directors has included such names as Jeffrey Immelt, Diane Sawyer, Peter Borish, Marie-Josee Kravis, Lloyd Blankfein of Goldman Sachs, Richard S. Fuld, Jr. formerly of Lehman Brothers, Glenn Dubin, of Highbridge Capital, Marian Wright Edelman, and Gwyneth Paltrow.

- The Veteran Jobs Mission is dedicated to finding employment and career development for U.S. military veterans, co-founded by JPMorgan Chase in 2011 a coalition of more than 235 companies. Collectively, members of the Mission are committed to hiring a total of one million veterans.

- The Council for Economic Education is the leading U.S. non-profit organization promoting financial education for students, from kindergarten through high school. CEE is more than 70 years old and its support is led by corporations such as Ford, Wells Fargo, and PWC. Each year CEE now trains 55,000 teachers who in turn reach approximately 5 million students throughout the country.

The broadest, most inclusive business alliance promoting CSR globally is the UN Global Compact. More than 13,000 organizations in over 170 countries have CEOs who engage through the compact on UN initiatives, including visionary leaders such as Paul Polman of Unilever, Richard Branson of Virgin, Francois-Henri-Pinault of Kering, and Mo Ibrahim of Syntel. All 13,000 member CEOs and their employees have signed on to principles-driven business practices that grow their enterprises while pursuing the United Nations' list of 17 Sustainable Development Goals (SDGs) by 2030.[19]

Here again is a fairly easy, turnkey solution for the beginner or midway CSR practitioner to engage his or her company in potentially transformative CSR initiatives with little more than a signature for starters. It is astonishing to note how much goodwill, resources, knowledge, and talent in the world is already focused on addressing our greatest societal and planetary challenges. And it is all there for your consideration.

CEOs have emerged as the most critical players in global progress when it comes to CSR. If your CEO is seen as actively engaging with CSR activities, however small, employees are more likely to follow his or her lead.

Marc Benioff, CEO of Salesforce, founded the company with the simple idea of what he called a 1-1-1 philanthropic model. The company commits 1 percent of its equity, 1 percent of employees' time, and 1 percent of its product to nonprofit work. "As the CEO," he says, "I need to embrace all of my stakeholders, not just all of my shareholders. What I'm trying to do is maximize stakeholder value. My goals for the company are to do well and do good. The most important thing to me is that we bring along all our stakeholders with us."

That simple idea of 1-1-1 evolved into a cause called Pledge 1%, for which thousands of companies have signed on to that same level of across-the-board commitment. Benioff is among a new breed of activist CEOs who are willing to stand for causes that reflect the values of their employees, customers, and other stakeholders. These new age CEOs at companies such as Google, Apple, PayPal, and Tesla are not purely focused on shareholders but instead on all major stakeholders. Employees, regulators, media, elected officials, non-governmental organizations (NGOs), and other influencers are now factored into the CEO's strategies and messaging.

When in 2014 the state of Indiana passed a new law that permitted discrimination against LGBT individuals, Benioff was the first CEO of a major company to cancel all corporate events in Indiana and halted plans to expand in the state. Salesforce is Indiana's largest tech employer, so the impact was felt in the legislature and elsewhere. The Indianapolis Star ran a front-page editorial with headlines that screamed "FIX THIS NOW." An amendment to the law protecting LGBT rights subsequently passed.

Benioff believes this activism strengthens his company. "As we've done that," he says, "our employees get a much higher level of satisfaction and fulfillment, knowing that they work for a company that supports that." Salesforce remains a highly profitable company that is regarded as one of the fastest growing software companies in history.

A dramatic example of industries and companies getting together to produce an amazing result, showing the real power of CSR when everyone pulls together, occurred in the spring of 2015 in North Carolina.

On March 23, Governor Pat McCrory signed a controversial LGBT bill known as HB142 or "The Bathroom Bill" into law, essentially directing transgender citizens to which bathrooms they could use. Companies with strong CSR commitments to equality and inclusion, as well as government officials, universities, and prominent newsmakers came out staunchly against the measure. And a number of groups and individuals, often conservative or religiously affiliated, have come out in favor. The new law limited legal protections of LGBT individuals by setting a statewide definition of protected classes of citizens.

More than 100 top executives from major companies, including major Charlotte employers like Bank of America, signed a letter opposing the "anti-LGBT" legislation. The NBA, set to host its 2016 All-Star Game in Charlotte, also opposed the measure. A who's who of leading corporations came out in protest, including Fox, Hyatt, Ingersoll-Rand, American Airlines, Bank of America, the NBA, YouTube, Google, Pfizer, Cisco, IBM, and more.[20]

The uproar and changes in office-holders from the 2016 election cycle resulted in a compromise deal in March 2017, ridding the most well-known provision of House Bill 2 that required transgender people to use restrooms corresponding to the sex on their birth certificates in many public buildings.

Emergencies like the discriminatory Indiana and North Carolina laws set the stage for what happened when President Trump announced he was pulling the U.S. government out of the Paris Climate Agreement. Signed in 2015, the agreement aims to curb climate change before the global average temperature reaches a point that scientists say would have catastrophic and irreversible effects on the planet.

In rapid order, hundreds of companies, along with 80 university presidents, 30 cities and a handful of states announced they would continue to abide by the Paris Agreement, no matter what the U.S. government planned to do. Billionaire philanthropist Michael Bloomberg is leading the group and is developing plans with the United Nations to commit businesses to greenhouse-gas limits set in the Paris Agreement. CSR leaders such as Google, Hewlett-Packard, Mars, and many others are stepping up to address a significant planetary challenge. And their employees and customers are right there behind them.

Industry Advertisement Challenging 2017 "Bathroom Bill" in North
Carolina

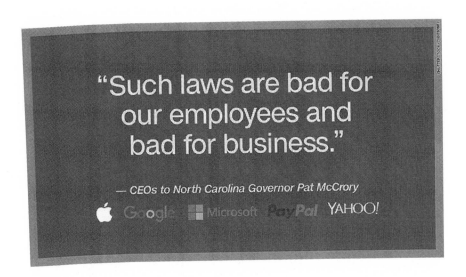

What this signals is that nation states perhaps are being eclipsed by companies (and cities and states) as the real players when it comes to global sustainability. It is happening now because it is the right thing for them to do, and it is what their employees and their customers want for the planet.

CHAPTER FOUR
Iterate

"If at first you don't succeed, you're running about average."
– M.H. Alderson

It never hurts to try. That is true for most things in life, but it is especially true in a fast-evolving field like CSR.

Back when we just beginning to plan the 2010 Green Auction at Christie's, I recalled reading a wonderful article about how the Obamas were interested in adding more diverse artists and genres to the White House art collection. The story gave me a thought: We had just begun developing our list of Green Auction patrons and supporters. Wouldn't it be epic if the Obamas were on that list? The fact is that it would be great to have anyone from the White House participating in the auction.

I made a cold call to 1600 Pennsylvania Avenue, and I was connected with the office of Desiree Rogers, then the White House Social Secretary and the first person of African-American descent to ever serve in that role. I followed up with a note inviting Mrs. Obama to visit us anytime at Christie's, and to consider being our honorary host of the inaugural Green Auction. I referred to the news story I had read as a pretext for writing, noting the Obama's stated interest in expanding the White House collection.

What followed for the next six months was a series of emails going back and forth, with the White House never saying "yes", but more importantly, never saying "no". The possibility of the First Lady's participation really helped keep our committee inspired and excited. It reminded everyone that we were up to big things. When we reached out to potential patrons and supporters for the auction, we were not shy about telling everyone that our Green Auction was being considered for involvement by the First Lady.

When our invitation was finally declined, we were disappointed, though we always knew it was a long shot. Although Ms. Rogers left the White House not long after, we continued to keep open communications with the staff in Social Secretary's

Office. I actually sent them a gift set of the Elizabeth Taylor Collection catalogues, which may well be in an archive somewhere. Eventually, we also secured recognition for Christie's by the President's Volunteer Service Award.[21]

There is magic in throwing yourself into an effort of this kind, even those with the smallest, most unpredictable chances of success. As many of my CSR colleagues have heard me often say, "momentum is our friend." I really do believe this. The simple fact is that many successful efforts take two or three attempts before they produce the desired result. Countless times I have encountered difficulties and setbacks that tempted me to give up trying on a given project – only to try again and prevail. Just keep moving forward.

In many of those cases, our early disappointment later proved to be absolute necessary to our ultimate success. We learned valuable lessons early on that improved our efforts on the second or third attempt and helped shape the final result. Once you have experienced how disappointment is essential for effective re-iteration, you can experience disappointment without getting too frustrated. Even at the darkest moments, we learned to interpret every "no" as a "maybe."

So the question is not whether or not to try again. The need to try again (and again) should be expected. The question is, how to try again, how to re-think, re-adjust or take a new path. On everything you attempt for the first time, you should not only expect setbacks, but welcome them. Setbacks tell how you are doing and what you need to move forward.

In that way each challenge will lead to further innovation and experimentation. As you develop your CSR program, you will have ups and downs, along with the occasional Aha! moments. Those inflection points that will allow you to pivot and turn to and even stronger and more influential space. That will most likely make your program stronger and engage more employees.

4.1. No workplace is perfect

The four pillars of Christie's Art + Soul program are environment, philanthropy, volunteerism, and thought leadership. For a variety of reasons, the environment proved to be the weakest of the four when I was there. That was a shame because employees were almost unanimous in their desire for a strong environmental component to our CSR program. Given the nature of Christie's business, even minor progress on the environment proved difficult, so we started small and made gradual, cautious steps.

We began by working with our Facilities department and our heroic London colleague Giles Mountain to measure our consumption of energy and water, as well as our output of waste. We could not possibly work with all 50 or more offices from the start, so we focused on our three largest salerooms: New York, London, and Hong Kong.

We soon learned that when it came to greening our workspaces, our hands were somewhat tied because many of Christie's offices are leased spaces in which the landlord decides how electricity, water, heating, and waste are managed. In our Rockefeller Center New York offices, for example, our attempts to sort and recycle waste were thwarted because the building maintenance crew simply dumped all sorted trash into a single bin each evening. The only solution we could come up with was to raise consciousness about where all our waste was going. We created an investigative report that culminated in an infographic that depicted the journey of our office waste to a sorting center in Queens, where fully 95% of all of our waste was indeed recycled.

In London, where we owned and managed our facilities, we could be bolder. We instituted waste-sorting in individual departments and removed all under-desk baskets, forcing employees to sort their waste into larger collecting areas and thereby educate them to the amount of waste they helped generate each day. We were careful to prepare employees for the switch, and with enough advance notice it went over fairly smoothly.

We also did away with Styrofoam coffee cups and disposable plastic water bottles. In their place, we provided coffee mugs and elegant water carafes for still and sparkling water. We also installed small galley kitchens with filtered, on-demand hot and cold water, and dishwashing machines so dirty mugs would not pile up in the sink. Each and every cup and carafe was imprinted with the Christie's logo, so we reduced plastic waste while inspiring pride in our brand. Overall, we were proud of the approach, though disappointed that we could not replicate it in worksites where Christie's was not the landlord.

At the same time, we worked with our corporate travel agent to track our air mileage, in order to help us get a baseline measure for our total carbon footprint. "Business getting," an elegant English turn of phrase for what Americans call sales or business development, can be rough on the environment. Jetting around the world to meet with prospective clients is an absolute necessity in this high-touch industry, where a single client's artworks can sell for tens of millions of dollars. Christie's millions of annual air miles ranked among its top three contributors to its carbon footprint.

Airlines and large companies have led the way in measuring their carbon footprints and then "offsetting" their impact with environmental projects that absorb the carbon dioxide they have created. JetBlue has partnered with Carbonfund.org for almost a decade and has offset more than 1.5 billion pounds of carbon dioxide through a variety of projects. One such project funded the planting of 25,000 trees in the Angeles National Forest in southern California, following a 2013 wildfire.

And yet, carbon offsets are also somewhat controversial. How do we know they work? Are we paying for something that would have happened anyway? And how do we know if several clients are paying for the same project several times over and over? We talked over all these issues, researched the competing providers of carbon offset solutions providers, and made our best choice.

In 2015, our 9.4 million passenger-miles were responsible for an estimated 2,380 metric tons of carbon dioxide. We wrote a check out of our CSR budget so that our carbon offset provider could invest in a pond at Green Valley Dairy in Wisconsin. Then we published a photo of the pond in our annual CSR report, so that all our stakeholders can see how we have chosen to be responsible for our impact on climate change.

Did I wish and work for greater reduction of Christie's carbon footprint than this? Of course I did. There are some in the company who no doubt wish we flew less frequently, but the fact is that face-to-face meetings are essential to the company's well-being. Cutting down on waste is a good thing, but "business getting" is what business is about – and Christie's business getting will always require a significant number of air miles.

True CSR requires keeping companies healthy enough to be socially responsible. Perhaps as newer airliners become more fuel-efficient, we might influence our companies to favor the airlines, such as Singapore Air, that choose to fly those planes. We already see that trend developing in the trucking industry. Zero-emission semi-trucks designed by Tesla and other companies have attracted lucrative pre-orders from Anheuser Busch, Walmart, Pepsi, and other companies anxious to reduce their carbon footprints. These vehicles are hardly a single solution to global warming, but they may prove to be an important incremental step to displacing millions of tons of diesel fuel emissions.

This is how CSR keeps evolving, by simultaneously creating environmental progress and new pro-environment business opportunities. It may not be long before companies begin writing into their CSR policies that they will only do business with shippers using zero-emissions trucks. Fear of losing out on those accounts might inspire trucking companies to begin abandoning diesel-engine semi-trucks in their fleets. All these effects contribute to a gradual switch, which we were already seeing, away from carbon-based energy sources and toward clean, renewable energy.

It is this common-sense inevitability about the direction of change that makes CSR such a thrilling field to be in. As you encounter the occasional deflating setback and disappointment, it is helpful to remember that the wind is at our backs, helping us move ever forward. Our job in CSR is to keep pushing ahead, wherever and however we can. By creating small wins within our own companies, we contribute to CSR's unpredictable evolution. The CSR campaign is ongoing.

4.2. Volunteering ups and downs

As noted in the previous chapter, today's employees expect their companies to provide them with access to volunteering and other philanthropic activities. Turning this desire into opportunities for your colleagues can be time-consuming work that necessitates a lot of trial and error. Volunteerism was our true home run at Christie's, but even there we faced headwinds and some difficult choices.

Volunteer time off (VTO) is an important starting point for expressing the company's commitment to CSR. So it was important for me to begin our volunteer efforts by convincing our CEO to agree to offer 8 hours per year of VTO as a part of our full-time employee benefits. (Eight hours per year has become a fairly dependable standard for VTO). About 60% of the world's largest companies offer VTO, but surveys in the U.S. of all employers put the number much lower, around 2%.[22] Armed with the facts and data, we were able to quickly secure VTO as an employee benefit – a significant achievement for our CSR.

Having made the case for VTO, we next faced the challenge of encouraging employees to actually use their time off and record their volunteer activities. We promoted the use of online tools offered by VolunteerMatch and did our best to communicate volunteer opportunities that were convenient and consistent with our employees' skill sets. By year one, we had about 25% of employees participating, which is a success by most measures, but since I am my own worst critic, I noted our shortcomings.

One thing I wished for was more participation from our top executives. That would have set a positive example and inspired a greater rate of participation among their direct reports. On the other hand, the active volunteers that we did attract were outstanding. They really took to the new ethos within our organization, and by the second year, a handful of them had taken on board responsibilities at various non-profit organizations. Their activities raised our team spirit and gave employees more reasons to feel Christie's was a good place to work.

Once we had attracted volunteers among about one quarter of our colleagues, we needed to do something more to get the next 25% on board. If you are doing it right, you are always raising the bar of accomplishment for CSR. David Stangis, chief sustainability officer for Campbell's Soup Company, has written how "CSR practitioners [need] to be on their toes – constantly learning...leaders are expected to deepen their business acumen, political savvy, and negotiation skills daily."

To attract more volunteer activity, we sought to infuse our company culture with a spirit of volunteerism through an annual Arts Assembly volunteer fair that allowed prospective volunteers to meet with representatives of local non-profit organizations in New York.

We rapidly discovered that our small staff could not possibly accommodate all the non-profits that wanted to come to Christie's and put themselves on display for volunteer opportunities. We were a team of two full-time employees and two interns – so we had to make some tough decisions.

We could barely process the 20 organizations that we had initially attracted, so for year one we drew the line there. Then, in order to be strategic and consistent with our cultural orientation, we chose to invite visual arts organizations only, excluding the performing arts. We also favored organizations nearer to where our employees reside (e.g., Manhattan, Brooklyn, and Queens) in order to encourage continued engagement with the organizations after the assembly.

Then, on the day of the new event, we had to remind ourselves not to squander the opportunity by hoping some employees would simply show up and sign up. That, we realized, would be akin to throwing spaghetti at the wall and hoping it would stick. So we really walked the halls and promoted our event. That effort helped us improve attendance and also take suggestions for making improvements.

Food and beverages are absolutely necessary for supporting a fun atmosphere at such events, and we happily discovered that given the charitable orientation of the event, my incredibly capable deputy Katelyn Norris and consultant Karen Zornow Leiding were able to wrangle free beverages from some really great local coffee and juice shops.

As we got to know the cohort of non-profit leaders who attended our event, we learned that they were keen to not just win volunteers, but they also wanted to learn best management practices from a global business such as Christie's. For the second year of the Arts Assembly, we introduced a luncheon for a candid and instructive discussion around best practices in human resources. Our guest of honor was Paul Richardson, Chief Diversity Officer of The Walt Disney Company and head of Human Resources for ESPN, as well as Christie's own phenomenal global head of Human Resources, Kerry Chandler.

We did a quick round of introductions with everyone asking their one biggest question. I framed it as "What keeps you up at night?" And then I kept notes and bucketed the questions into larger thematic questions so that once we went around the table, our guest speakers were able to respond to a handful of questions that addressed each executive director's specific concerns. They not only got sage counsel from industry experts, they also had a new network of peers to bounce ideas off of to collaborate with.

The cost of this event was probably about $250, which has always served as a reminder that money, while welcome and often needed, also tends to be the least-creative solution to any challenge. CSR activities enable employees to accomplish something together, for a higher purpose beyond their work roles, and with a different mix of colleagues than what their regular responsibilities call for. They get to know each other differently and better. They get a bit of a break from their daily routines, and infuse their day with a bit of a spiritual lift. Each time you engage them in a volunteer exercise, solicit feedback real time or shortly afterwards to see what resonated with them and then bake their feedback into your ongoing efforts, always iterating.

When natural disasters strike, however, giving money is indeed what the moment calls for. We struggled to meet our employees needs in this respect. Particularly when disasters took place in regions where we had significant numbers of employees or clients, we never found a simple way to really financial support behind a sudden urgent cause. We also really had no philanthropic budget to use for these purposes.

In a similar vein, we were never able to get a successful global matching gift program launched. Our only matching gift program was in the U.S., and only for matches of up to $200 per employee per year. We never could ask that the program be expanded because the annual budget set aside for such matches was never fully used. I believe we still managed to create an atmosphere of giving, but it was more of a feel than an actual global giving practice, which arguably is better than having done nothing at all.

In retrospect, we could have promoted the U.S. matching program more thoroughly, but instead we expanded our energy and resources trying to identify global solution for all employees. I consulted with my CSR network to try and find what other multinationals were doing in the area, but we were never able to find an easy off-the-shelf solution that would work across borders. Particularly in countries with strict privacy practices or those with lack of philanthropic traditions, it is still a challenge for multinationals to have a one-stop solution for employee matching gift programs. If I had to do it again, I would have focused exclusively on raising the U.S. participation rates and made sure the annual budget was completely used up. The lesson I learned, is that it is much better to hold back your expenditure of time and political capital toward wider program expansion until after you have first demonstrated overwhelming evidence of program success and popularity at a micro level.

4.3. Learn from others' mistakes

In April, 2017, Pepsi released a two-minute-39-second ad described on its YouTube channel as "A short film about the moments when we decide to let go, choose to act, follow our passion and nothing holds us back." In the video, celebrity model Kendall Jenner is seen posing in a blond wig at a photoshoot, when a peace protest marches by. She impulsively ditches her wig, grabs a can of Pepsi and joins the protest. When she makes her way to the front of the march, police in riot gear are blocking the way. Jenner walks up to one police officer, hands him her Pepsi, and as he drinks it, the crowd erupts in cheers.

The negative outcry against the video was immediate and savage. It was derided for trivializing police brutality protest movements like Black Lives Matter. Bernice King, daughter of Martin Luther King Jr., drew 290,000 likes with her sarcastic tweet, "If only Daddy would have known about the power of #Pepsi." The Independent newspaper in Britain called the Pepsi ad "possibly the worst commercial of all time." The social media commentary reportedly left Kendall Jenner in tears.[23]

After just a few days of being pilloried on social media, Pepsi pulled the ad. A press release stated that, "Pepsi was trying to project a global message of unity, peace and understanding. Clearly we missed the mark, and we apologize. We did not intend to make light of any serious issue." A writer for Wired magazine responded with the facetious observation that the ad, "did indeed provoke conversation – about Pepsi's tone-deafness…. The reaction to Pepsi's ad, not the ad itself, brought people together. That's refreshing."[24]

The previous chapter touched on the risks of combining CSR with marketing (greenwashing, clumsy advertising, product gimmickry, awkward corporate donations or off-message sponsorships). The Kendall Jenner ad certainly seems like one of those off-message errors in judgment. Showing a TV star defusing a potentially violent standoff with a single can of soda was a comically bad way to convey a message of "unity, peace, and understanding."

But the real underlying problem with the Pepsi ad involved collaboration, or lack thereof. It is not a coincidence that this video was produced by Pepsi's in-house branded content studio. Brad Jakeman, the PepsiCo executive who helped develop and run the studio, claimed: "It just becomes more efficient at some level to have it in-house."[25] (Jakeman announced plans to leave Pepsi not long after the hubbub subsided.)[26]

However, doing so limits the feedback to the content producers and in this instance allowed the release of such a tone-deaf video. Marketing experts noted at the time that collaborating with outside advertising agencies helps companies avoid this problem. As one agency executive wrote, "You want the people making content for you to challenge your assumptions. Because if you breathe only the stale air inside your very own content farm, you might find yourself apologizing to Kendall Jenner, and to all of America, one day after you hit 'send' on your 'rendered creative.'"[27]

Embarrassment can be a useful wake-up call for accountability and authenticity within a company's culture. It is not enough to claim good intentions. Social responsibility is in the eye of your beholders – your customers, neighbors, employees, suppliers, partners, shareholders, and other investors. Over time, companies that survive these kinds of messaging mishaps get wiser and more responsible.

As a general principle, collaboration helps you avoid mistakes in the planning phase and it buffers the blow when things go wrong. For these and other reasons, it is smart for the head of CSR to coordinate closely with counterparts in departments such as marketing, public relations, government relations, corporate giving, and investor relations. You get invaluable feedback regarding all possible questions or challenges prior to launch, and then there is a shared sense of ownership for projects after the launch – which helps ensure their success.

The video caused little lasting damage to Pepsi's brand. A strong underlying CSR culture, which Pepsi has, allows brands recover from these hiccups very quickly. Consumers are willing to give a brand the benefit of the doubt if a lapse in judgment really comes across as an aberration, not a pattern, which was the case with Pepsi. When a brand genuinely invests in CSR, it inoculates the brand to some degree from these kinds of mistakes.

Six months after the infamous Pepsi ad was taken down, Dove products was forced to remove an online ad for body wash that many interpreted to have a racial subtext. A Dove spokesperson said the company would be "re-evaluating our internal processes for creating and reviewing content."[28] Dove's already-strong CSR program will be stronger now because of this incident.

Dove's official comment hints at the underlying sources of resistance to collaboration: you have to submit what you do to review of others. The one unavoidable downside of collaboration is that you do not always get your way.

I think back to my own participation in the Cultural Property Committee at Christie's. It was a cross-functional team that included representatives from Legal, Communications, CSR and the art specialist departments. We grappled with issues such as authentication challenges, restitution of Nazi-looted artworks and dealing in conflict antiquities from Syria and Iraq. It was a great, smooth-running team under the strong leadership of General Counsel Martin Wilson, and it grew through a collaborative process that was disciplined and scaled up.

However, I recognized that this consensus-oriented process fostered policies that were more cautious and conservative (from a CSR perspective) than I would have preferred. For example, I was a supporter, without success, of a Christie's moratorium on the sale of all objects with ivory in them.

In accord with the international treaty on trading in endangered species, Christie's and other auction houses will not deal in artworks that are known to have "contemporary" ivory in them. Christie's has gone further to educate around the topic of rhino and elephant poaching, for example working on a lecture series with the Tusk Trust, a charity whose patrons include Prince Harry and Prince William.

A growing number of wildlife organizations, however, are advocating a complete ban on selling ivory of any kind, including antique altar pieces, pianos, and other decorative art objects that may have small pieces of ivory inlays. The belief is that trade in this "antique ivory" supports the demand for new ivory. More than 30,000 elephants are killed each year for their tusks, and a 2016 census estimated that the population of savannah elephants had dropped by 30% in the previous seven years.[29]

For months, our Cultural Property Committee researched and debated the question of banning antique ivory. Although only a tiny portion of Christie's sales contain antique ivory, the fear was that we might be forced to reject handling a major collection just because of a few antique ivory items in the collection. I advocated for a moratorium – a pause on dealing in all ivory for one or two years – while we studied the effect on our sales, on our competitors, and whether we had any effect on the overall horror of poaching. To my mind, the moratorium would give us a unique opportunity to define common ground on the issue, having seen and evaluated the issue from multiple perspectives. But this was not the view that carried the day. The policy allowing sales of objects with antique ivory remains to this day.

Ultimately, CSR cannot possibly be accountable for all business practices. Progress in CSR often emerges from sudden jolts in the marketplace caused by public embarrassment or scandal. There may come a time when all auction houses are forced to cease sales regardless of their concerns about sales. In such circumstances, when a company is suffering the headache of scandal or loss of market share, CSR can help the company set a new course. Never forget that CSR can help repair customer problems created by other areas of the organization.

The Volkswagen emissions scandal is a case in point. In 2015 the U.S. Environmental Protection Agency filed a formal complaint charging Volkswagen engineers with using engine software to circumvent emissions limits on their diesel engines. In normal traffic, cars made by Volkswagen were emitting far more pollutants than was legally permissible. When the cars were being tested for emissions, a code in the engine software detected the testing pattern and adjusted the engine so it ran cleaner and at a lower level of performance.

In the resulting fallout to this scandal, Volkswagen has pleaded guilty to conspiracy to defraud the U.S. government and paid out more than $20 billion in fines and settlements. In December 2017, Volkswagen's U.S. chief of engineering and environment was sentenced to seven years in prison, while eight other Volkswagen executives were indicted. In Germany, Volkswagen's CEO resigned, two Volkswagen executives were charged, and another 50 were put under investigation. By 2018, other investigations were ongoing in countries all over the world.

Under a new CEO, Volkswagen's 2016 CSR report revealed an enormous course correction at the company due to this terrible scandal. The report reads in part, "Painful experience, especially the massive loss of trust that followed the diesel issue, has made it clear that when it comes to integrity, our primary aim must be to become a role model for a modern, transparent, and successful enterprise."[30] Among many changes to corporate governance, the company's board of management now reserves a seat for one "Board Member for Integrity and Legal Affairs."

As far as its product offerings are concerned, Volkswagen has stopped selling diesel vehicles in the U.S. and has accelerated its pace in developing to zero-emissions electric vehicles. Prior to the scandal, Volkswagen had been a notable industry laggard in making electric cars. Volkswagen's latest five-year plan calls for investing around $40 billion toward making Volkswagen "number one world-wide in electric mobility by 2025." The company is planning $85 billion in total direct investment in electric and other new car technologies by the end of 2022.[31]

Finally, out of its legal settlement agreements in the U.S., Volkswagen agreed to provide $2 billion in funding toward a subsidiary called Electrify America, which will use that settlement money through 2026 to build a coast-to-coast network of fast-charging electric-car charging stations. More than 2,800 charging stations will be installed in the 17 largest U.S. metropolitan areas by 2019. "There hasn't been a significant catalyst yet for ramping up the number of charging stations," notes Scott Fisher of Greenlots, a Los Angeles-based contractor for Electrify America. "This is an unprecedented opportunity to help create the electric vehicle infrastructure we need across the U.S."[32] Without the Volkswagen emissions scandal, there is no telling when or how such a network would have ever taken shape.

The irony is that Volkswagen has long had a very strong CSR program, reaching into all aspects of social responsibility, not just the environment. The scandal brought on by its engineers (and covered up by top executives) has suddenly made CSR (and the company's leaders in CSR) central to the company's return to both profitability and respectability. The Volkswagen scandal has cost the company so much money in fines, settlements, and depressed stock prices that it has also raised red flags among global companies and their investors. They recognize how Volkswagen's CSR, had it been stronger, might have prevented the company's shameful emissions scandal, at a cost of $20 billion and growing.

Whether your company is an old manufacturing firm or a new digital start-up, your long-term success – true sustainability – requires you to expose your business practices proactively to the world – declared, shared, and independently audited. Then let others – customers, employees, investors, regulators, and the media – confirm or deny that you are a responsible business worthy of their engagement.

4.4 Never Stop Taking Chances

Where will the new focus on electric vehicles lead Volkswagen? It is impossible to say and that is why it is so important to keep trying new things. You do not know where they will lead.

Our whole Art + Soul initiative at Christie's grew out of a single annual event, our Green Auction, begun in 2010. I was able to cajole and inspire a forward-looking group of business and nonprofit leaders to collaborate in a three-year commitment for a charity auction to benefit four environmental groups. The unprecedented collaboration, Bid to Save the Earth, was bold and created something out of nothing, thanks to a team of amazingly talented and inspired individuals.

From the start I knew that a good way to begin an event of this kind was to have a preset termination date. Fundraising events have a shelf-life in my experience, and three years is a pretty good date to quit and start over with something new. A sunset date for a new project gives everyone a view to a gracious exit. Open-ended commitments make people nervous, as they should. Who wants to be the bad guy if the thing does not work and you have to pull out? It is much easier to make a three-year commitment, so you are never in the embarrassing position of having to pull out.

To create Bid to Save the Earth, we were creating something from nothing, with no precedent. It seemed at every turn there were obstacles:

- There was no budget, and it was not clear where the budget should come from;
- We needed a new, separate 501C3 charitable organization to hold the funds that would ultimately be divided amongst our four partner not-for-profits;
- Our accounting and auction systems software did not allow for a hybrid auction with multiple beneficiaries;
- Our area specialists had limited time to devote, because they were all focused on their standard sales and clients' needs; and
- Our company culture was driven by commercial success, not charity.

There was resistance everywhere, which is to be expected in anything worth doing. (If you are attempting something that would happen anyway, where is the achievement?)

So I had to convince countless colleagues to dream big and begin to see charity through our clients' eyes. My colleagues were well aware that most major art collectors are also active in various charities and philanthropies. A big charity auction would be a unique way to engage our existing clients and build relationships with prospective clients.

Then-CEO Ed Dolman understood the concept and supported it from the start. He had come up through the ranks of Christie's, and his nose for business was combined with a moral compass that points north. He knew that charity was important to many of our most enlightened and successful clients, such as Lily Safra, Steve Cohen, Leonardo di Caprio, Princess Margaret, and Li Ka-shing.

Even with CEO support, I still had to sell the concept to my colleagues. I had countless conversations on this subject, many of which ended with non-committal shrugs. A key in such conversations is to always hear your colleagues' concerns and offer responses that will help them feel more comfortable crossing the finish line with you – even if they are not true believers. Again, remember to assume the positive attitude of a veteran campaigner and know that every "no" today really means "maybe" later.

We agreed to that we should work with a handful of environmental organizations that also captured the "time, treasure, and talent" of our top clients. In so doing, we were integrating our charity auction into the core of our business development strategy. I started to research and engage four non-profit organizations one at a time.

I knew that we needed to meet three basic criteria. We had to choose a globally compelling cause. We needed to partner with a handful of world class charities. Specifically, 4-star rated by Charity Navigator, the leading rating website for not-for-profits. And we needed to choose charitable partners whose patrons included major art collectors. I would be calling on each organization individually to convince them to join our effort. We settled on:

- Oceana, with my pal and confidant the author, environmentalist and philanthropist Susan Cohn Rockefeller (among other notable collectors) on its board;
- Conservation International, with such stellar leaders as Howard Schultz and Harrison Ford among its trustees;
- The storied Natural Resources Defense Council and its powerhouse president Frances Beinecke and intrepid development head Pattie Sullivan; and

- The Central Park Conservancy, given the park's renown and the Conservancy's leadership team which included dynamo CEO Doug Blonsky, development chief Terri Coppersmith, and noted art collector and trustee Patsy Tarr.

All of these charities compete with each other for donor dollars. Essentially, I needed to convince them, one organization at a time, that linking arms would generate a collective lift and a greater upside than if they passed on the opportunity. I need to build a community – a movement really – to create what ultimately became the highly acclaimed A Bid to Save the Earth.

I turned to my closest pals and past collaborators to help me through this difficult task. These included Sue Rockefeller and fashion scout and sustainability guru Julie Gilhart of Barney's, plus my Christie's colleagues Cathy Elkies, Karen Gray, and Lydia Fenet. And I tapped some great influencers including Jennifer Schwab of Sierra Club Green Home and NBC Universal CSR officer Beth Colleton.

With our four beneficiaries signed on, I implemented weekly conference calls to get our army moving toward staging the event. Collectively we harnessed networks and resources to secure a $50,000 sponsorship from Deutsche Bank, media sponsorship from Target and plenty of celebrity guests including Salma Hayek Pinault, members of the Rockefeller family, and comedian Chevy Chase as our emcee.

We secured artworks from leading artists and even auctioned off a round of golf with former President Bill Clinton, all for the environment. By the end of the first year, we raised nearly $700,000 for the four charities and earned tremendous media visibility.

We repeated the project in years two and three, with no funds from Christie's but with lots of in-kind support, buoyed by the desire to raise the company's profile. By our final year, year three, we decided to go out with a bang. With the help of Vogue's Sylvana Ward-Durrett, Virginia Smith and Megan Salt, Vanity Fair's Graydon and Anna Carter and Sara Marks, and Christie's powerhouse charity auctioneer Lydia Fenet, we secured then rising rap star Nicki Minaj as our entertainer. Rappers strutting their stuff in leather bustiers had never been seen before at Christie's fine auction house in Rockefeller Center. That kind of fare is not common at most gala charity events in New York. But we took the risk, in part because it was the final year. We were rewarded with plenty of buzz, funds and joy.

The relationships begun during the three years of the Green Auction helped to launch what became Art + Soul, and those relationships continue to benefit Christie's. Iteration year after year made the Green Auction stronger and better. I personally continue to benefit from the bonds formed during those three years.

The lesson I draw from these years of ups and downs is that every project has a positive impact, even if it is minimal or hard to recognize in the moment. What you do is important, and it does help advance society and the planet, even if not at first as much as you might wish. It is important to remember this. Even if the immediate results are modest or seem to be in vain, if you dream big, collaborate and build in the fun factor to all that you do, you always have the chance to build new relationships and prepare to greater victories down the road. And you will go to sleep at night knowing that you made a positive difference in the world.

All along the way, sharing the risk makes it a bit easier when things go wrong, and sharing the rewards makes success all the more joyful.

Nicki Minaj at Christie's Green Auction, a charitable event followed by a fashion show at Rockefeller Center, in March 2012. Credit: Lucas Jackson/Reuters

CHAPTER FIVE
Measure What is Material

> "In God we trust; all others must bring data."
> – Jack Welch

Bloomberg is one of the world's largest privately-owned companies, with 19,000 employees and 176 locations on 6 continents. The information and technology company regards itself as "the central nervous system of global finance." It was built by founder Michael Bloomberg under the credo, "If you can't measure it, you can't manage it."

Bloomberg's annual CSR report reflects this belief in the power of measurement. In 2013, the company announced its 2020 target metrics for CSR activities in three areas: People, Products, and Planet. Each year's report documents Bloomberg's progress toward those specific measurable target achievements.

Results reported in Bloomberg's 2016 Impact Report[33] included:

- People – In 2016, more than 11,000 employees dedicated over 128,000 hours of volunteer service in 74 cities around the world. Ninety percent of employees engaged with at least one volunteer group (reaching the participation goal for 2020) and 49% engaged with two or more.

- Products – In May 2016, Bloomberg launched the Bloomberg Financial Services Gender-Equality Index (BFGEI), a first of its kind index that measures the performance of financial service companies recognized for supporting both data disclosure and best-in-class policies and practices in the gender-equality space.

- Planet – In 2016, Bloomberg joined RE100, a global initiative businesses committed to 100% renewable electricity by 2025. Bloomberg's 2020 goal for all carbon emissions is a 20% reduction from the 2007 baseline.

In 2009 Bloomberg acquired a company called New Energy Finance, which provides information services regarding the renewable energy markets. The company subsequently launched Bloomberg ESG Data Service, which collects ESG data for over 10,000 publicly-listed companies. Bloomberg now rates companies each year based on their ESG data and then integrates that data into Bloomberg Equities and Intelligence Services, allowing investors to gauge how well companies are responding to their ESG challenges.

The evolution of a mainstream financial company like Bloomberg into these areas shows how CSR has emerged as a source of substantive concern for managers and investors alike. Whether nobly inspired or not, the business community is now measuring, reporting and executing ESG strategies with the assumption that they are important reflections of corporate health and sustainability. The loop is now closing with employees, customers and outside influencers now supporting those brands that execute well on a triple-bottom-line basis.

Fittingly for someone who built an empire on his faith in measurement, Michael Bloomberg chairs the previously mentioned SASB, the Sustainability Accounting Standards Board, the industry-led initiative aimed at improving the quality and usefulness of sustainability information. As Bloomberg has noted, "No company can solve sustainability challenges alone. The more that join this growing effort to measure and share climate risks, the faster we'll make progress."[34]

5.1. Measuring CSR Impact

The measuring of CSR for investment impact is one of the surest signs that CSR is destined to melt into every company's entire value proposition. This means that the measuring system you develop will set the stage for your future efforts around CSR. Having a strong measurement methodology will reinforce your case on every effort you make. It will also help you choose where to double down and transform your company's levels of ESG expression and commitment.

For instance, in 2017, Kering, the previously discussed Paris-based parent company for luxury brands such as Gucci and Saint Laurent, announced a plan to reduce the company's environmental footprint by 40% by 2025, and set quantitative targets with specific KPIs (key performance indicators) to track the progress.

"There must be a clear strategy, with clear, specific targets, just as you have in the financial side of the business," says Marie-Claire, Kering's chief sustainability officer and head of international institutional affairs. "To change a paradigm, you must have a long-term vision, so we are speaking of 2025."

In most cases, you will be pleased to find that you already have a CSR measurement practices already in place. For example, if your company has a matching gift program for employees, the financial systems will already have a line item for those contributions. If the company has standing commitments to equal opportunity employment practices and goals, you can include that information in your CSR report.

For other CSR projects, you can begin the task of measuring and tracking them with the help of KPIs related to these four basic measures:

- Inputs
- Outputs
- Outcomes
- Impacts

With this simple model, for example, the relevant KPIs for our Christie's Arts Assembly volunteer fair would include:

- Input KPIs: staff time, cash budget and in-kind contributions;
- Output KPIs: numbers for attendance, participation and sign-ups;
- Outcome KPIs: numbers of people who joined boards, number of hours they and how many hours they have devoted hours to non-profit work; and

- Impact KPIs: numbers and related narratives that tell how our Christie's employees made a difference serving on these non-profit boards.

This process helps you draw a critical distinction between outcomes and impacts. Basically, a CSR outcome is about your company. A CSR impact is about your stakeholder.

For instance, if your company installs high-efficiency lighting as a part of a sustainable energy initiative, the reduced dollars spent on electricity is an outcome. The avoided pounds greenhouse gases entering the environment is the impact.

Measuring outcomes is always easier than measuring impacts – but impacts are what matter most. Impacts are material to CSR success, and you always want to measure what is material, even if that is sometimes a serious challenge.

To use Christie's again as a convenient example, we measured the outcomes from our volunteer charity auctions ($170 million in 2015) and from the dollars we raised on behalf of clients who sold collections to benefit their favorite charities ($250 million). All these outcomes, with dollar totals and the names and types of organizations that benefited, were duly noted in the annual CSR report.

However, to give our stakeholders the full sense of our CSR program impact, we needed to paint a picture of how those dollars made a difference. So our annual CSR report was filled with images and graphics showing how our work impacted stakeholders within all three circles of our bullseye target. For instance, we showed how a new community-based art education curriculum made the lives of community members better, and how it helped improve the neighborhood where it was located.

"We've found social media platforms to be very effective tools for sharing impactful content, like photos and videos of the people who have benefited from CSR programs," says Tae Yoo, who leads CSR for Cisco. The company recently released a series of videos on Instagram, Facebook, and Twitter about several non-profits the company supports with cash grants and product contributions. "We wanted to highlight the great work they do, using the power of social media, which led to incredible results. In addition, it catalyzed thousands to take a more in-depth look at these inspirational people and organizations."

In general, impacts are narrative, while outcomes are numerical. Impact stories of this kind are vital for breathing life into what are otherwise cold and quantitative outcome metrics. It may take a little more work and imagination to tell the story of your CSR impact. But it is worth it. The way an employee's life is affected by volunteering can be incredibly powerful – and it is something that can best be communicated through that employee's personal account.

The ultimate goal of metrics is to inspire more good work of this kind. And to inspire people, it often takes both quantitative outcomes and qualitative impacts – numbers and narratives. Your employees, customers, and investors want KPIs for CSR that offer an objective, uniform, and rigorous progress report from one year to the next. But they also want to hear the voices of people who benefit from your work. Those are the people who provide first-hand evidence of your CSR impact.

This focus on impact can also be invaluable at the planning stage of any new project or program. To assess the potential value of a CSR initiative, think first what constitutes a desirable impact from the stakeholder's perspective. Then you can figure out the necessary KPIs by walking them backward. Begin by asking what would success look like from the beneficiary's perspective? Next, what outcomes would we need in order to achieve that impact? Then, what outputs need to be generated to achieve those outcomes? Finally, what kinds of measurable inputs – investments of time and money – would be needed to achieve all these results?

By making these choices about what to measure and how to measure it, you get the chance to consider what is truly material to your CSR success. From there you can set benchmark goals for coming years and assess your own year-to-year performance. This much is certain: New ideas will keep coming at you, much faster than you possibly handle. Given your limited time and resources, how can you choose which projects to take on and which ones to let go if you do not have metrics and a process to help you decide?

5.2. Integrated ESG Reporting

Global companies have been hit in recent years by a series of disasters in areas of their operations where ESG compliance was sorely lacking. Consider how giant corporations such as BP, Volkswagen, Wells Fargo and many others have had their valuations damaged by management practices in areas as diverse poor environmental controls, unethical sales inducements, mistreatment of employees by suppliers, and unchecked sexual harassment by top managers.

Go back a few decades and consider how events such as the 1984 Union Carbide pesticide plant spill in Bhopal, India, the 1989 Exxon Valdez oil spill in Alaska, and the 1998 Tobacco Master Settlement in the U.S. federal courts exposed tragic indifference to social responsibility among the leaders of major corporations. They also exposed the limits of traditional financial reporting in preventing such catastrophic events from destroying shareholder value.

Among investors, there is a growing awareness of how ESG accountability is needed to reduce such risks to their holdings, and that companies with the very highest ESG reporting standards can be bundled into portfolios of low-risk social impact funds.

Leading companies have responded by moving toward ESG reporting that is integrated with their financial reporting. They are incorporating ESG information into all their communications with investors and other players in the financial markets.

I recommend this route for all companies because not only does it improve transparency and accountability within the company, but once these ESG reporting practices are established, it becomes easier each year to complete the report and enhance ongoing efforts.

GRI, the Global Reporting Initiative, might be considered the lingua franca of ESG reporting. Its guidelines enable organizations of any size, type, sector, or geographic location to evaluate their impact on issues such as climate change, human rights, and corruption. More than 8,000 companies globally are using GRI to share the results of their CSR efforts alongside of their financial reporting.

A sound approach is to use GRI to identify the key drivers that would appear in your company's report, and then take note of what public companies in your industry or sector are doing along these lines. An enormous library of GRI reports is available for review at the UN Global Compact website (UNGC.org).

Two other common measurement systems are tailored more directly to the investment community:

- SASB, the previously noted Sustainability Accounting Standards Board, sets standards designed to be included in mandatory financial filings with the SEC and other regulatory bodies. There are now distinct sets of SASB standards covering 79 different industries across 11 broad sectors of the global economy.

- The IIRC (International Integrated Reporting Council) sets standards with a slightly different focus. There is greater emphasis on how CSR practices add shareholder value and offers the company a sustainable, long-term approach to its growth.

Private companies and small and midsize enterprises should not feel obliged to prepare CSR reports that would meet the rigor of SASB or IIRC. Complying with rigorous SASB and IIRC reporting standards could prove to be onerous and overwhelming for a small CSR team within a private company.

On the other hand, there are several good reasons for smaller companies to integrate ESG reporting as a routine part of their regular financial accounting. Consider that public companies are getting increasingly choosy about whom they qualify as partners and suppliers. Leading companies in CSR might need to see your ESG report before considering doing business with you. For instance, if your company ever wants to raise capital or prepare for a buyout by a public company, adherence to these reporting standards will come up as a positive sign of your company's financial soundness during due diligence.

Some 50,000 companies of all sizes have benchmarked their CSR progress with the user-friendly B Impact Assessment tool, sponsored by the non-profit B Lab. The assessment takes two-to-three hours to complete. After submitting your report online, you will be able to see how your company measures up against 40,000 other companies that have their results on file. Then you can create an improvement plan with best-practice guides, all for free.

About 2,100 firms have taken a further step and used this same tool to achieve official B Corp certification. These certified B Corps, from 50 countries and 130 industries, work with B Lab to meet rigorous standards of social and environmental performance, accountability, and transparency. Familiar industry leaders who are certified B Corps include Patagonia, Eileen Fisher, Warby Parker, The Honest Company, Ben & Jerry's, Etsy, and Hootsuite.

B Corp certification can be used to redefine the very nature how the organization measures success. In more than 30 U.S. states, B Corp designation (also known as "public benefit corporation" status) is recognized legally, which protects B-Corps from shareholder lawsuits asserting that the company has a fiduciary duty to only maximize profits.

"The purpose of this firm is not to create shareholder value," Danone CEO Emmanuel Faber told The Economist in 2018. Danone has pledged to become a B Corp, and its U.S. subsidiary, DanoneWave, has already become the largest public benefit corporation in the world. "A public benefit corporation is managed in a way that balances shareholders' financial interests and the benefits it brings to people, the planet, and broader society," Faber wrote in 2017. "We are not perfect, but the movement has started already, and we are ready to drive it further."[35]

5.3. Communicating Your Results

The UN Global Compact has developed an exceptionally useful online tool called the Value Driver Model, which can help you assess and communicate the financial impact of your CSR strategies. The model uses common business metrics to illustrate how corporate sustainability activities contribute to overall company performance in three basic areas:

- Growth – Revenue growth from sustainability-advantaged products, services, and strategies.

- Productivity – Total annual cost savings (and avoided costs) from sustainability-driven productivity initiatives.

- Risk Management – Sustainability-related reductions in risk-exposure that might otherwise impair the company's performance.

The Value Driver Model allows you to design metrics that describe the connection between sustainable practices and company value creation. It can be tweaked to accommodate various ways of expressing profitability, whether its return on equity (ROE) or return on capital employed (ROCE), which is often favored in capital-intensive industries and sectors.

The Value Driver Toolkit simplifies the task of applying this model to your own strategies, operations, and communications. Available at the Compact's library, the toolkit also includes helpful case examples and model training presentations.[36]

Discussing your results with all your company's stakeholders is a final step, one that is essential to continual CSR improvement. You need to develop feedback systems for each of the audience groups and sub-groups within your CSR bullseye target – fellow employees, company brass, customers, suppliers, and members of your community.

For these purposes, I personally favor one-on-one conversations, or small group consultations. However, social media and polling resources such as SurveyMonkey can also help you develop fast feedback from many sources. If you make it a point to deepen your understanding of the motives, goals, and needs of your various stakeholders, you will be in the best position possible to select the metrics that are most worth tracking. By grasping what your stakeholders value most, you will maximize your beneficial impact in the areas you seek to serve.

Select the metrics, data, and stories by choosing to report on what your stakeholders value most. In that sense, measuring the success of sustainability efforts is necessarily an ongoing work-in-progress. As sustainability metrics become more advanced, companies are increasingly measuring and communicating impact, giving them the ability to review how CSR efforts benefit their community and the bottom-line. And with that as your aim, you build feedback systems that fit your particular organization structure and culture.

"We regularly conduct extensive research to validate that we are investing in the right areas, where we can provide the most value add, and have the greatest potential for impact," says Tae Yoo, Senior Vice President of CSR and Sustainability at Cisco. In the 2017 fiscal year, Cisco reported cash and in-kind contributions equivalent to 2.89% of company earnings (measured as EBIT, before interest and taxes) and were able to positively impact over 154 million people, as reported by their nonprofit grantees.

Bringing measures and transparency to CSR makes it easier for all stakeholders to recognize the company's role in its community and its industry. Using these tools and metrics can also help contribute to a desirable workplace culture of accountability and focus on results. In that way, effective CSR measurement can improve the company's operations in some unexpected ways, sometimes with a transformative impact on the company.

In 2009 Bank of America merged with Merrill Lynch. "We saw this as an opportunity" notes Andrea Sullivan of Bank of America Merrill Lynch. "We looked at our company closely and began the journey of embedding responsible growth in to every aspect of our organization. Over the years we have continued to enhance our ESG leadership, creating a supportive workplace, and a responsible approach around risk management and business opportunities. This strong culture has enabled us to better serve our clients, strengthen our communities and deliver added value to our shareholders."

Additionally, by setting clear goals and measures for diversity and philanthropy, a company can unlock areas of talent and skills that management had been previously overlooked. When companies measure their waste output, they can seek markets for that waste, so it is not wasted.

The story of the Real Dill, a small Denver-based pickle company, provides a simple example of how this can work. When the company's founders experienced a season of explosive sales growth, they became very self-conscious of how much waste they were creating. Each week, they were bagging up hundreds of pounds of trimmings from cucumbers, horse radishes, and peppers sending it all to landfills. At the same time, gallons of cucumber-flavored water were going down the drain each day as a byproduct of the pickling process.

"It just got to the point where we were feeling so guilty about that," co-founder Justin Park told Fast Company magazine, referring to the cucumber water. "It is a byproduct, but it tastes incredible, and we figured there had to be a better use for it."[37] That simple insight led to the launch of The Real Dill's Bloody Mary Mix. Made with cucumber water otherwise destined for the drain, the Bloody Mary mix rapidly became The Real Dill's best-selling product.

The company founders solved their waste problem by having a local community gardening group cart away their scraps each week for use as compostable material. All 500 pounds of The Real Dill's weekly food waste (12 tons per year) now goes toward helping increase yields in local vegetable gardens and farms.

"For us, it felt like a win," Park said. "We're keeping these scraps out of the landfill, and putting them in the hands of an organization that's using them for good…Whatever minimal responsibility it creates for us is completely worthwhile."

The larger the company, the more profound the impact of metrics can be. When the Chinese e-commerce giant Alibaba began studying and tracking the breadth of its impact on the economy, new opportunities for CSR opened up. The company launched an internal research division, AliResearch, which estimated that Alibaba Group's retail marketplaces had contributed to the creation of over 15 million job opportunities for people working directly for online storefronts and for service providers to Alibaba merchants. Research also revealed that approximately half of the active sellers on Alibaba's China retail marketplaces were female.

That insight has led the company to join efforts to foster gender parity and workforce inclusivity. The company developed programs to expand equal opportunities in other areas, such as a cloud customer service program designed for people with disabilities, and an enormous project called the Rural Taobao partnership, which encourages ecommerce development in China's vast impoverished rural areas.

Alibaba has announced plans to invest $1.6 billion toward the opening of 100,000 Rural Taobao centers to help facilitate local trade. The partnership has leveraged significant resources from the government, which has spent the equivalent of $300 million in 200 rural counties toward training, warehouse construction, and other supporting activities. According to one Alibaba representative, "when we send in one Alibaba employee, the government deploys 10 people."[38]

In a wide variety of ways, the powerful Alibaba ecommerce platform has been turned into a platform for doing good. Merchants on Alibaba can designate percentages of their sales proceeds to charitable organizations, and consumers can contribute to charitable causes through product purchases or by participating in online charity auctions. Charities can raise funds and engage volunteers through their own Alibaba Group storefronts. (In 2016, Alibaba facilitated approximately 3.3 billion charitable donations involving more than 280 million consumers, 1.5 million merchants and 230 million yuan.)

Alibaba also used its platform to raise the equivalent of $30 million in donations for more than 60 environmental causes in 2016, involving The Nature Conservancy, National Geographic Air and Water Conservation Fund, Paulson Institute and Institute of Public and Environmental Affairs. Alibaba has become a model of CSR success, showing how a company can use its assets, expertise, and advanced analytics to integrate ESG solutions with its business model.

5.4. The rise of the ratings

In 2016, the U.S. market for ESG-related sustainable, responsible, and impact investment products was $8.72 trillion, or one-fifth of all investment under professional management. That marked a 33% increase since 2014 and growth in the sector is ongoing.[39]

Capital markets are now helping drive an accelerating movement toward more transparent and responsible business practices. Private sector employers are adding socially responsible investment fund options to retirement plans. Under the visionary leadership of president Darren Walker, the Ford Foundation has committed $1 billion of its endowment to mission-related investments. Money managers and institutional investors are scrutinizing an ever-expanding array of concerns – including climate change, testing on animals, human rights, income disparities, gender equality, and safe working environments.

The Dow Jones Sustainability Index (DJSI) was launched in 1999 as the first global index of the leading sustainability-driven companies, sorted by industry sector. The results serve as a kind of annual pulse-taking of global ESG trends. For instance, in 2016, a review of the results showed the area of greatest improvement was corporate citizenship, and philanthropy, while the area of least improvement was labor practice indicators and human rights. Some of the top companies in their sectors for the 2016 DJSI included LG

Electronics, Abbott Laboratories, Sodexo, BMW, UBS Group and Nestle.

As asset managers, financial institutions, institutional investors, and others rely on ESG ratings to help them make investment decisions, ratings by third-party firms such as Bloomberg ESG Data Service are growing increasingly important in determining its access to investment capital.

The Harvard Law School Forum on Corporate Governance and Financial Regulation has produced a handy guide comparing the many ratings firms,[40] but one firm worth a special mention is RepRisk, because of its large scope. The company provides ESG reports for more than 84,000 private and public companies in 34 sectors around the world. Companies qualify for a RepRisk rating by participating in the firm's data verification process.

Through these rankings and ratings, we can see all sizes of companies linking their businesses to higher purposes such as education, environment, and poverty reduction – because employees, customers, clients, and investors all expect this from them. The loop is now closing with employees, customers, and outside influencers now supporting those brands that execute well on a triple-bottom-line basis. The rise of social impact investing has further underscored this rising consciousness – awakening the sleeping giant so to speak – that is business. Now the ultimate investment opportunity is the company that yields great financial returns while also advancing society's well-being and leaving the smallest possible footprint on the planet.

5.5. How CSR metrics can shake the world

If your company becomes a CSR leader within its industry or within its community, it is worth considering how you can extend the use of your internal metrics for the common good, and enhance your reputation among some of your most important customers, suppliers, and other stakeholders. Certain companies have been able to use their access to metrics and measurements within their particular industry niches in order to create new standards that can help create a shift in progress that can ripple throughout the world.

Aviva, the British-based multinational insurance company, joined with a number of partners in 2017 to launch the first Corporate Human Rights Benchmark (CHRB), assessing 98 of the largest publicly traded companies in the world on 100 human-rights indicators. The effort represents a unique deployment of the company's core competency, which is customer assessment and underwriting.

CHRB is divided into four key industrial sectors (agriculture, apparel, extractives, and information and communication technology). The ratings are designed to harness corporate competition within each of those sectors to encourage continuous improvement in human rights performance.

By 2020, Aviva intends to expand the ranking to cover the world's top 500 public companies. "It will seek to assess the reality behind companies' public commitments," says John Morrison of the Institute for Human Rights and Business, "including what they do to address negative impacts when things go wrong, and what kinds of collaborations they undertake to scale their resources."

Transparency and competition are proving to be powerful tools in driving a "race to the top" in a wide variety of CSR areas. Oxfam's "Behind the Brands" initiative has created competition among ten major food and beverage conglomerates to eliminate rural land grabs, enhance the status of women in their supply chains, and reduce carbon emissions. Similarly, the "Access to Medicine Index" has prompted the pharmaceutical industry to increase access to medicines for poor people suffering from HIV/AIDS, tuberculosis, and other treatable illnesses.

In a similar way, SAP Ariba, the subsidiary of German technology giant SAP, has turned its metrics technology into a tool to disrupt illicit human trafficking and forced labor practices.

"SAP Ariba's main business is saving customers money through their supply chains, tracking over $1 trillion in business-to-business transactions every year. In 2015, the company partnered with the international non-profit Made In A Free World to bring labor transparency to its global cloud-based network.

Padmini Ranganathan, Vice President of Products and Innovation at SAP Ariba, told TechRepublic, "We need to not just focus on cost and profitability, but also focus on the good and the impact this can generate. We can generate momentum in business, we help create that impact – not just cost, but impact."

Experts estimate there are an estimated 20 million to 30 million forced laborers in today's global economy. By helping its customers monitor and report on their procurement and related ESG issues, SAP Ariba has created a "good-conscience marketplace" where buyers and sellers enjoy transparent views of each other's labor practices in areas such as manufacturing, fishing, and cotton and cocoa production.

Companies in these kinds of pivotal industry positions can magnify their CSR impact significantly by invoking common third-party metrics as minimal compliance standards for the companies they do business with.

Swiss-based UBS Bank, for instance, is a model CSR company in many ways. The Dow Jones Sustainability Index ranks it in first place in its diversified financials industry group. The DJSI ranking cites UBS's innovative financial products and regards the firm's GRI reporting as "exemplary." Around 30% of UBS employees were engaged in volunteering in 2016, which added up to 18,386 workers expending 155,325 volunteer hours.

However, UBS expands the impact of its CSR significantly by screening potential clients and business suppliers for activities that violate ESG standards. For example, the bank refuses to provide credit or conduct transactions for companies involved in making or selling cluster munitions and anti-personnel mines. UBS also rejects companies that violate standards of behavior set by a wide variety of international organizations, including UNESCO and the International Labor Organization Convention. Before doing business with UBS, companies must be audited for their impact on:

- World heritage sites (UNESCO)
- Internationally significant wetlands (UNESCO Ramsar Convention)
- Endangered species (CITES: Convention on International Trade in Endangered Species)
- High-conservation-value forests (Forest Stewardship Council)
- Child labor (International Labor Organization's Conventions 138 and 182)
- Forced labor (International Labor Organization's Convention 29)
- Indigenous peoples' rights (International Finance Corporation's Performance Standard 7)

Finance is the lifeblood of business. When financial firms like UBS refuse to lend money raise capital for companies with poor ESG performances, then CSR becomes mission-critical to every company's survival. The trend is clear. As CSR becomes increasingly easier to measure and compare from one company to the next, socially irresponsible companies will find it increasingly difficult to remain viable in the Caring Economy.

CHAPTER SIX
The Campaign is Ongoing

"Keep Calm and Carry On."
– British World War II Motivational Poster

In an interview in early 2017, Mark Zuckerberg told Fast Company magazine why Facebook does not engage in corporate philanthropy.

"A lot of companies do nice things with small parts of their resources," he said. "I would hope that our core mission is the main thing we want to accomplish: making the world more open and connected. Almost all of our resources go toward that."

At the time, Zuckerberg expressed the belief that Facebook's work was inherently socially responsible because Facebook helps people connect with each other. To his mind Facebook had no need to "give back" because for Facebook doing more business and doing more good was the same exact thing.

That attitude might help explain why Facebook was completely unprepared for the storm of criticism it met with during the investigations of the 2016 Presidential election. As more details came to light about how Russians used fraudulent Facebook profiles and Facebook ads to influence voters, Facebook's advertising practices were shown to encourage anti-social behavior. Facebook algorithms reward advertisers whose content produces high rates of "engagement," which meant that during the presidential campaign, "fake news" that made outrageous claims was much cheaper to distribute than more responsible political messages. Inflammatory ads that pushed scandalous lies and racist content received deep discounts from Facebook because they were so widely shared.

By June of 2017, a chastened Zuckerberg announced Facebook was throwing out its founding mission statement. Its original goal of "making the world more open and connected" with replaced with a new mission, "to bring the world closer together." He pledged to redouble the company's efforts to rid the social network of "bad actors" and shift its focus towards creating communities instead of dividing people against each other. "I used to think that if we just gave people a voice and helped people connect, that would make the world a better place by itself," Zuckerberg said. "Now I believe we have a responsibility to do even more."

The announcement did not do very much to stem the tide of criticism. Facebook's leadership was slow and clumsy in its response and gave the impression it could not cope. Facebook's first president, billionaire entrepreneur Sean Parker, said he now regrets having been a part of promoting Facebook in its early years. "I don't know if I really understood the consequences of what I was saying," he said. "God only knows what it's doing to our children's brains." Calls went out from the investment community that the time had come for Zuckerberg and his team to step aside.

For the first time, there were suggestions that Facebook needed to fall under government regulation. Marc Benioff compared the social danger of all social media to that of cigarettes. Senator Dianne Feinstein lectured the lawyers for Facebook and Twitter, "You have a huge problem on your hands. And the U.S. is going to be the first of the countries to bring it to your attention, and other countries are going follow…because you bear responsibility. You created the platforms…and now they're being misused. And you have to be the ones who do something about it – or we will." The company's former privacy manager wrote an op-ed stating that the government needs to step in because, "The company won't protect us by itself, and nothing less than our democracy is at stake."

The turmoil at Facebook is just one example of how rapidly shifting concepts of social responsibility can overtake a company. Mass shootings in 2018 challenged big retailers like Walmart and Dick's to question the social responsibility of selling weapons designed for war to civilians. At almost the same time, the women's #MeToo movement prompted widespread evaluations about how sexual harassment complaints have been handled in the workplace. At many companies that led to policy changes that addressed hiring, promotions and pay practices that tend to put women at a disadvantage.

These events serve as vivid reminders that CSR is in a state of constant evolution, and that it is worthwhile to keep your eyes open to changes on the horizon. In this chapter I note some of the foreseeable trends that may be stirring up even greater changes that what we have seen in recent years. Many of developments discussed in this book were almost unimaginable five or ten years before they attained mainstream status. What are some of the bright ideas and social trends will determine the shape of the mainstream in 2025 and beyond?

Today's CSR community is so sophisticated and professionalized that it would seem to be up to the challenge of change. The danger, however, is that CSR is also becoming a self-referential community, with a cottage industry of consultants, software solutions, and industry associations producing commercialized and generic answers to complex problems.

CSR is becoming institutionalized, and institutions of all kinds tend to be slow to change and rarely ask hard questions about their own usefulness. As a CSR leader, your task is to resist the temptation to tick off various boxes for CSR compliance while ignoring future changes lurking around the corner. When filling out this year's CSR report for your organization, consider what might be on the edge of possibility for next year's report, and for the year after that.

6.1. The future of work

As Baby Boomers retire and the Millennial generation moves into increasing positions of authority, a new generation nicknamed Generation Z began entering the workplace in 2014. They are young people born after 1997. Their attitudes resemble those of the Millennials in many ways, but they are even more independent-minded and less deferential to authority. The 2009 recession hit when many of them were children, and they have grown up in an economic recovery marked by anxiety. They are true natives of the Internet and the global economy. They know nothing else.

Employers face some peculiar challenges with this workforce. Millennials and Generation Z are career nomads willing to move to another job if they do not feel their workplace offers them a sense of purpose and treats employees fairly. Two different polls in 2016 came to the same conclusion about people under 30 – roughly half of them have a negative impression of capitalism. They do not espouse support for socialism, either, but their daily experience of the free market leaves them cold. It strikes them as unfair, inhuman, and deprives too many people of their basic needs.

Google counts among the leading companies when it comes to addressing these kinds of concerns. The company has expended $1 billion in grants and one million employee volunteer hours in support "to create more opportunity for everyone." Google is also funding efforts toward greater economic mobility. Google is funding organizations that are using technology and innovation to train people with new skills, connect job-seekers with high-quality jobs, and support workers in low-wage employment. It invested $50 million with grantees such as Goodwill, the leading workforce development organization in the U.S. With a $10 million grant and 1,000 Google volunteers, they launched the Goodwill Digital Career Accelerator to enable 1.2 million people across the U.S. to learn and expand their digital skills and career opportunities.

Similarly, in Germany, Turkey, and Jordan, Google is working with Kiron to bring digital skills training to refugees through a combination of online study and partnerships with local universities. And in France, they are funding Bayes Impact to improve and scale their open-source software that uses big data and machine learning to generate personalized job search recommendations, so that people can find quality jobs that match their skills. Google has granted millions of dollars to nonprofits dedicated to fighting bias and prejudice, such as the Equal Justice Initiative, the LGBT Center in New York, the Stonewall National Monument, and the Institute for Strategic Dialogue in the UK, which fosters innovation in countering extremism and hate groups, both online and offline.

Google's workplace culture encourages employees to express themselves through internal email lists, even if it means challenging each other's work or criticizing the company's products. It's another reason why Google is a top-ranked workplace among Millennials, but the practice has led to some very public battles of words in the media. A male computer programmer was fired after posting a long manifesto critical of Google's diversity efforts, declaring that women are biologically ill-suited for writing computer code. Another Google worker was fired for lashing out on the email lists against co-workers posting messages that he felt were expressing white supremacist views.

But when more than 3,000 Google employees signed a letter protesting the company's involvement in a defense department project, it had an impact on top executives. An employee town hall was convened, and Google's Cloud chief promised that no more defense-related projects would be undertaken until the company drafted a new set of ethical principles to guide its work. Tellingly, the executive apologized for contracting to do defense work before any such principles had been established.

That was yet another case of younger employees awakening top executives to new realities. If it can happen to a top-ranked employer like Google, it can happen to anyone. The only way to avoid such crises is to consult with employees beforehand, at a level of inclusion and transparency that few companies are currently comfortable with. For instance, annual meetings at the staid old Washington law firm of Nixon Peabody now include everyone, not just partners. And when a design committee was formed to help determine the layout of the firm's new offices, attorneys, paralegals, and receptionists were included.

The ideas contributed by younger employees defined the new space. All offices are the exact same size – for senior partners, as well as junior associates and paralegals. Each office has glass walls to spread light throughout the floor and, according to the Washington Post, "to signal transparency, democracy, and connection." Corner spaces, which were once the coveted location of high-status partner offices, were designed as team meeting rooms.

Andrew Glincher, Nixon Peabody's chief executive told The Post, "Several years ago, the attitude of law-firm partners was,

'Millennials are going to have to be like us.' But very quickly, they learned, they're not going to be like us. And we need to adapt. We need to be open to new ideas and keenly aware of what motivates Millennials. Especially if we want to attract and retain top talent."

The success of Nixon Peabody's redesign began with its process of consulting everyone, and making everyone feel heard. Not everyone understands that the values cherished by younger employees includes being consulted about what those values should look like in action.

The Mars Corporation, one of the largest private companies in the world, provides some excellent models in the area of staying in touch with worker sentiment in a sizeable organization. The company employs Gallup, for instance, to run its Mars Annual Engagement Survey to measure employee engagement levels and probe for danger areas in need of improvement. An ombudsman program provides "a confidential, neutral, and alternative channel of communication for associates to report workplace issues or concerns." All of Mars offices have open-plan designs, and the values of transparency and collaboration are repeated throughout its many corporate communications. Above all, Mars expresses faith in its employees: "Our Associates know our business the best – we trust them to tell us if something isn't working."

The Mars company does a lot of listening to employees because the only way to know for sure that employees feel they are being treated fairly is to ask them in a wide variety of ways. As more and more employees arrive at the workplace expecting to derive a sense of equality and purpose in their roles, employers should expect to keep raising the levels of transparency and freedom of expression beyond what was common in the past.

Pay transparency has emerged in recent years as a gender equality issue, as a way of ensuring that the company is not secretly paying women less. But way back in 1986, Whole Foods founder John Mackey foresaw the sustainability benefits of opening the book's everyone's salary. He wrote in his book, "The Decoded Company," "If you're trying to create a high-trust organization, an organization where people are all-for-one and one-for-all, you can't have secrets."

Experimentation of this kind has been going on for years since, especially among technology firms. Buffer, a social media management company, practices a form of radical pay transparency in which all salaries and the formulas used to determine those salaries are openly available on the company website.

The practical objective is to attract and retain employees with shared values. As Buffer co-founder Leo Widrich wrote in his blog, "One day, I interviewed an engineering candidate and I asked them 'Why do you want to work here?" and he said, "Because I know more about your company, than the company I currently work for. That's why I want to work with you!'"

Pay transparency is not a passing fad. It is a growing trend that is emblematic of the new generation's general mistrust and skepticism about traditional management practices. Traditional top-down hierarchical structures are giving way to "self-organizing" work structures that are more agile and adaptive to unpredictable change. The exercise of control in the workplace is trending towards forms that that are more transparent, informal and collaborative. Values such as openness and freedom of expression are valued – and even necessary – in such "self-managed" organizations.

The term "holacracy" has emerged to describe a form of organization that is both "holistic" and "democratic" in its power structure. Inspired in part by proven models of collaborative workplaces such as engineering "skunkworks" and agile software development, workplaces employing the holacracy model make leadership opportunities to everyone, forsaking older models that emphasize seniority and rigid reporting relationships.

The most prominent company to reorganize under holacracy is the online shoe retailer Zappos. There are no job titles and no managers dividing up the work in top-down silos at Zappos. Instead, fluid teams called "circles" respond to tasks that need to be done. Each employee might have a number of roles within several circles, instead of being slotted in single job title within a department.

Zappos employees are expected to lead and act as a problem-solving entrepreneur within their circles. Each of them surrenders that degree of security and power that comes from having a distinct job title. What they get in return is what Millennials and other younger workers say they value most – a sense of meaning and purpose in their daily work. Employees see a fuller view of the company and have the flexibility to contribute in ways that reflect their talents and passions. The daily focus is on constant improvement, and decision-making happens without the deadening pull of approvals and paperwork in hierarchical bureaucracies.

There are almost 100 companies on six continents employing holacracy today, with the larger examples including Heavenly Nutrition in Indonesia, the Social Innovation Academy in Uganda, Business School Lausanne in Switzerland, the U.S. insurer Mylo, the Dutch online retailer bol.com, and Tochka, a Russian financial services firm. Holacracy poses some unique challenges in terms of identifying the right compensation and finding employees who thrive in such an environment. Zappos CEO Tony Hsieh believes such challenges are worth overcoming, because holacracy is critical to Zappos's ability to adapt to rapid change in its industry. Quoting Darwin's Origin of Species, Hsieh points out, "It's not the fastest or strongest that survive. It's the ones most adaptive to change."

6.2. The future of commerce

Demonstrating a purpose beyond profit was a novel concept for consumer-oriented companies not so long ago. Now, with Millennials approaching their peak years of buying power, it takes a lot more to achieve distinction in the marketplace. As consumer expectations for CSR continue to rise, it is important to be aware of how leaders are finding the competitive edge when it comes to connecting with customers.

In Oakland, California, an office-supply company called Give Something Back states its mission right in its name. At its founding in 2008, it was modeled after Newman's Own, the food company launched by Paul Newman that gives away all its after-tax profits. Give Something Back donates nearly three quarters of its profits to local community organizations. Recipients are chosen using a balloting process that polls the company's 13,000 customers and 80-plus employees.

Give Something Back employs many of the obvious sustainable measures you would expect for a company that claims a higher purpose. The headquarters has a 50,000-watt solar farm on its roof. It offers a wide range of recycled and green products. It runs a toner recycling program. It takes in customers' old computers and other electronic devices, which it donates to a job retraining program.

What is remarkable, however, is that Give Something Back does not expect you to pay a little extra for doing the right thing. Instead it promises savings: "More than 50,000 products, all for less." A lot of retailers who offer sustainable products are forced charge a premium because they lack the scale of mass market competitors. That's not the case with Give Something Back. The company claims, "With lower overhead and smarter sourcing, our prices are consistently lower than the Big Box stores."

Give Something Back is now California's largest independent office supply company. The U.S. retail division of its main competitor, Staples, is struggling and closing stores while Amazon squeezes its online sales. Think about that for a minute. Is your organization ready for the day when a competitor is able to undercut your prices while also making customers feel they are helping others and helping the planet?

It seems like every day there are companies taking consumer brands in the direction of ever deeper meaning and importance. The nutrition bar company Kind Snacks was founded in 2004 by Daniel Lubetzky, the son of a Holocaust survivor with a passion for making the world a better place. Kind bars are healthy snacks that are easy on the planet's resources, but Lubetzky has taken Kind-ness to another level, invoking the company's name to promote a much higher purpose.

Lubetzky started his first enterprise, PeaceWorks, as a way to foster cooperation between Jews and Arabs in a sustainable business venture. The KIND Foundation has since founded an ambitious project called Empatico, which provides free video conferencing tools to help teachers connect their students to classrooms around the world.

Business-led efforts like these continue to gain traction and inspire because there is a growing consensus that larger sustainability initiatives have been declining in impact and relevance in recent years. Traditional institutions such as governments, universities, and foundations are increasingly seen to have fallen short on big issues such as climate change, social justice, and economic opportunity. These institutions keep launching new initiatives, but conditions are either not changing or they are getting worse.

In order to anticipate where new CSR leadership might arise, it is today's fringe players that are most highly motivated to become tomorrow's leading voices. China, for example, faces such a grave public health threat from air pollution that the government has instituted sweeping regulatory changes profoundly affecting emissions from manufacturing. China has also set a rigid schedule for phasing out cars with internal combustion engines – instantly making the company a leader in electric car technology.

And, despite being a nation with no tradition of formal philanthropic institutions or practices, China is seeing its new class of millionaires and billionaires creating countless new charities and foundations. In the coming decades, China may very well leapfrog Western philanthropy when it comes to CSR leadership, while its post-petroleum economy could lead the way in reversing climate change and reducing poverty.

Richard Liu, the humble but ambitious founder of China's second largest e-commerce giant JD.com announced in March 2018 that the company is ramping up efforts to establish logistics facilities in impoverished areas of China and build brands for local agricultural products to reduce poverty and hunger while generating jobs and business. The $64 billion company, traded on the

NASDAQ, is not even two decades old and it is revolutionizing commerce and CSR simultaneously.

Similarly, 19-year old Tencent Holdings, the world's biggest investment corporation valued at $600 billion now connects over one billion Chinese consumers daily through its WeChat social media platform. On September 9, 2015 the company launched Tencent 9/9 Charity Day, the number 9 being auspicious in Chinese culture. By September 2017, the annual campaign generated over $200 million in donations from the general public, its own foundation and social enterprises, all that benefited 6,400 charitable projects in the areas of education, medical assistance, poverty alleviation, and more.

New revolutionary solutions are arising from new technologies, and in places where needs are most acute. A U.S. foundation is testing the concept of a Universal Basic Income in Kenya, where payments via cellphone help with the viability of such an experiment viable. A high-tech system of intense greenhouse farming has allowed the tiny Netherlands to become the world's number two exporter of food. In the process, Dutch farmers have reduced their dependence on water by as much as 90%, almost completely eliminated the use of chemical pesticides and cut the use of antibiotics on farm animals by 60%.

Changes of this kind illustrate how entirely new ways of doing things may be needed to contend with the rising array of environmental, social and governance challenges facing the planet. The London-based consulting group Volans has reported, "There is a growing consensus that key parts of our current economic system are unfit for purpose in a world of 7-going-on-10 billion people by 2050." The firm's prescription calls for changes that represent breakthroughs in disruptive technologies, novel business models and what Volans refers to as "exponential mindsets." These are new ways of thinking that shift away "from an assumption that…sustainability is about slowing down and imposing costs towards seeing it as a matter of accelerating towards opportunities."[41]

This redefinition of sustainability predicts that companies that manage to move fast, find opportunities, and innovate are destined to become tomorrow's market leaders in their respective industries. A study of the UN's Sustainable Development Goals predicts that pursuit of those goals will generate $12 trillion in revenues and savings by 2030 in such sectors as health, agriculture, energy, and transportation.[42]

Among the many inspiring stories and handy tools on the Volans website, there is a downloadable presentation called "The Breakthrough Pitch: How to stretch the sustainability ambitions of business executives."[43] The document offers a step-by-step guide to making a case for sustainable business strategies that favor disruptive, exponential thinking over more gradualist solutions.

Novo Nordisk, a leading maker of insulin and other diabetes treatments, is held up as a model of breakthrough thinking. Although the company has profited from the rapid growth of diabetes cases around the world, the company has invested in diabetes-prevention measures, as well. In 2015, then-CEO Lars Rebien Sørensen told his employees, "If we wind up curing diabetes, and it destroys a big part of our business, we can be proud, and you can get a job anywhere."

6.3. The future of governance

Walter Isaacson's biography of Leonardo Da Vinci notes how the polymath's genius was nurtured and stimulated at the court of Ludovico Sforza, Duke of Milan, where "Leonardo found friends who could spark new ideas by rubbing together their diverse passions."

When it comes to managing change, there is strength in numbers and the regenerative creative energy that accumulates with gatherings of like-minded leaders. The world has shrunk considerably since the 15th Century, and the future of the planet now depends on business leaders challenging each other's imaginations, like the Milanese courtiers of long ago.

One great, star-studded point of collaboration right now is the B-Team, a small group of business leaders aiming to leverage the power of capitalism to create a sustainable future. Co-founded by billionaire Richard Branson and former Puma CEO Jochen Zeitz, the B-Team's membership includes Kathy Calvin of the United Nations Foundation, Francois-Henri Pinault of Kering, the luxury conglomerate, media entrepreneur Arianna Huffington, telecoms billionaire Mo Ibrahim, Ratan Tata of the Tata Group, and Zhang Yue, founder of Broad Group China.

On its website, the B-Team explains the origin of its name: "Plan A – where companies have been driven by the profit motive alone – is no longer acceptable. It's time for Plan B."

Implicit in that mission is the simple fact that the planet cannot be protected by a handful of companies practicing good global citizenship. The bar must be raised for all companies within the global economy. Among the B-Team's accomplishments:

- Helping launch a Global Beneficial Ownership Register with the aim of eliminating shell companies that are used to hide assets;
- Sponsoring the 100% Human at Work project to foster more humanistic work environments;
- Joining with the Natural Capital Coalition to develop a standard Natural Capital Protocol – a set of tools enabling companies to measure their impacts and dependencies on natural resources; and
- Encouraging a movement of entrepreneurs and business leaders called "Born B," committed to growing their companies from the outset with people, planet, and profit aligned.

The B-Team also lends its weight to more common sustainability efforts. In 2015 they advocated for an ambitious climate agreement at the COP21 meeting in Paris, and ten B-Team members have committed their companies, including Kering, Tiffany, Unilever, and Virgin, to reaching net-zero greenhouse gas emissions by 2050.

To my mind, the B-Team is a vital antidote to the threat that less responsible business poses to our society and our planet. It represents an inflection point, one in which a small group of powerful visionaries are settings new ethical standards of responsibility and marrying it with action. As the team and its work gains reputational currency and support, its appeal to the nobler ambitions of of a rising generation of customers and employees will help the team scale its solutions to very real and threatening problems.

The B-Team is a small and nimble group, which allows it totake action and make an impact without much deliberation.[44] On the other hand, if there is a down side to exclusive groups, it is that they risk becoming private clubs divorced from everyday reality. The B-Team's leaders are operating at a much higher level than their peers. If ordinary corporate governance does not make changes for the better, the B-Team's visions will remain only visions.

That is why I am so encouraged by the 2016 "Commonsense Principles of Corporate Governance," issued by an ad hoc group of U.S. business leaders, including JPMorgan, Berkshire Hathaway, Verizon, Vanguard, and BlackRock.[45] The signatories are not celebrities like Branson and Huffington, but they represent some of the world's largest asset managers, public pension funds, and mutual fund companies. These are the people who determine the massive flows of capital that can either kill or save the planet. It is notable that they see that fundamental change is needed in corporate structures to prevent us from continuing down a path to destruction.

Their set of common-sense principles recommend to boards call for transparency, diversity and an end to the destructive focus on short-term results over long-term sustainability. For example, their Commonsense Principles discourage companies from providing quarterly earnings reports unless those reports are beneficial to shareholders. They advocate for unfettered board access to the entire management team. And they reinforce the movement toward fuller diversity standards for governance.

The principles cover such governance topics as board composition, director responsibilities, shareholder rights, public reporting, board leadership, management succession planning, and compensation of management. Their ultimate emphasis is the importance of taking a long-term strategic perspective and avoiding trends, short-termism, and the nonessential.

Their principles are not pie-in-the-sky abstractions. They include these real-world measures that offer a preview as to what will be common practice in the not-so-distant future:

- No board should be beholden to the CEO or management, because truly independent corporate boards are vital to effective governance;
- Diverse boards make better decisions, so every board should have members with complementary and diverse skills, backgrounds, and experiences;
- It is important to balance wisdom and judgment that accompany experience and tenure with the need for fresh thinking and perspectives of new board members;
- Every board needs a strong leader who is independent of management. The board's independent directors usually are in the best position to evaluate whether the roles of chairman and CEO should be separate or combined; and if the board decides on a combined role, it is essential that the board have a strong lead independent director with clearly defined authorities and responsibilities;
- Financial markets have become too obsessed with quarterly earnings forecasts. Companies should not feel obligated to provide earnings guidance – and should do so only if they believe that providing such guidance is beneficial to shareholders; and
- Effective governance requires constructive engagement between a company and its shareholders. The company's institutional investors making decisions on proxy issues important to long-term value creation should have access to the company, its management and, in some circumstances, the board; similarly, a company, its management, and its board should have access to institutional investors' ultimate decision makers on those issues.

The full list of principles is available at GovernancePrinciples.org. The extraordinary thing about these "common sense" principles is that some of them would have been hard to imagine as mainstream ideas just a few years ago. CSR demands fundamentally different ways of governing, and it is likely no coincidence that the rise of CSR has been met with rising interest in socially responsible governance.

Thanks to CSR, many of these common-sense measures are now just catching up with the changing reality. It will not be long before boards lacking diversity will become as antique a business concept as switchboards and secretarial pools. BlackRock, the world's largest money manager, set a new standard in 2018 by stating that the companies in which it invests should have at least two female directors.[46] A number of state pension boards have threatened to cast negative votes against all boards with insufficient numbers of women and minorities. The New York Pension Board Fund, the nation's third largest, announced in 2018 that it will oppose the election of members to all-male boards. During the previous year, the fun owned shares in more than 400 U.S. businesses without any female directors.[47]

Equally problematic are companies governed by separate classes of stock, so that control of these public companies remains in the hands of just a few people, or even one person. The California State Teachers' Retirement System (CalSTRS) has claimed that Facebook's many problems are rooted in its dual-class stock ownership that gives founder and CEO Mark Zuckerberg 60 percent voting rights. "Why does Mr. Zuckerberg need the entrenchment factor of a dual-class structure?" asked a CalSTRS official. "Is it because he does not want governance to evolve with the rest of his company? If so, this American dream is now akin to a dictatorship."[48]

Facebook's issues point to the problem of a company fiddling with its mission statement and purpose without changing its management structure. "Any corporate purpose, however laudatory or noble that mission may be, must be accompanied by strong governance," writes Bruce Kiron, executive editor of MIT Sloan Management Review. "Even when managerial motivations are authentic, purpose without governance can go awry.... Purpose requires the steady hand of strong governance to assure that achieving a given purpose is done properly, within the boundaries of ethics and law."

GovernancePrinciples.org is a good reference tool for you to have your CSR toolbox as you drive your company's CSR journey. If you are on a corporate or non-profit board, it is good to take note of these developments. And if you are not, it is still a good idea for you to keep abreast of these developments so that you can design programs in line with their goals and also advise top members of your organization what is coming down the road. As the voice for CSR in your organization, you are quite naturally the voice for the company's future and its prospects for sustainable success.

CHAPTER SEVEN
Utopia

"We have to choose between a global market driven only by calculations of short-term profit, and one which has a human face."
– Kofi Annan

In November 2017, Roger Gifford, the chair of the UK's Green Finance Task Force noted that that the term "green finance" might be destined for obsolescence. Risk exposure due to climate change is becoming a widespread concern among lenders and investors. "From housing loans to venture capital and infrastructure investment," he wrote, "green means profits as well as climate risk mitigation. In this sense it is no different from regular finance – in time we won't even draw the distinction."

A similar observation has been made about LEED-certified building design. LEED (Leadership in Energy and Environmental Design) certification was once a somewhat rarified, high-end discipline. Now many aspects of LEED have become mainstream practice. LEED proponents say that was always the intent, for LEED to truly lead the entire design and construction industry toward sustainable development as a matter of course.

The path of these two CSR elements presage the inevitable integration of social responsibility into common business practice. All companies are destined to become be socially responsible in the near future, because socially irresponsible companies will find themselves isolated and unprofitable. They will be unable to attract customers, employees, suppliers and investors.

I have emphasized the importance of leadership in setting the course towards this goal. A future in which companies are truly responsive to the needs of all their stakeholders requires business leaders capable of being evangelists for the ideal of social responsibility. The word evangelist comes from the ancient Greek term for messenger (as does its root word, angel). Leaders who evangelize for social responsibility are able to communicate its message throughout the organization, moving everyone to action and mobilizing resources towards its goals.

In this final chapter, I want to leave you with what I think are the leading traits of a true CSR evangelist and offer some examples of leaders who embody this aspirations. They have all advanced their institutions closer to the normative standard – a newer, aspirational normal. The traits they demonstrate is not so much a to-do list as it is a reminder of what we would all be well served to aim for within our CSR.

7.1. Aim High
Pope Francis

Jorge Mario Bergoglio was installed as the 266th Pope of the Roman Catholic Church in March, 2013. He was the first to take the name Pope Francis, and shortly thereafter, he began to rock the world.

Pope Francis eschewed pomp and circumstance on the day he was elected, taking a bus back to the hotel with his fellow cardinals. Rather than live in the official papal apartment in the Apostolic Palace he moved into the simpler Vatican guest house where he could more easily receive visitors and hold meetings.

He encouraged priests to be more welcoming of gays and lesbians, divorced Catholics, and unmarried couples. He stressed the need for both the Church and society to give women and their concerns "more weight and more authority." And perhaps most importantly, he took personal responsibility for the Church's history of sexual abuse of children by priests, declaring, "I feel compelled to personally take on all the evil…to personally ask for forgiveness for the damage done."

As a Catholic by birth but lapsed in practice, the message of Pope Francis resonated with me. All Popes are evangelists, but this Pope is an evangelist for a more socially responsible (and more socially responsive) leadership in the Holy See. He aims to create more of a missionary church, one with less judging and more doing, less finger-wagging and more ministering. Within days I found myself moved to work with His Holiness, to seek a way to convene and connect in support of his mission.

In the autumn of 2013, I made my boldest cold call to date. I reached out to two contacts at the Vatican, proposing that they consider exploring a collaboration with Christie's, a global tour of selections from the Vatican Library and Vatican Museums. The tour, I wrote, "would be consistent with Pope Francis's democratization of the church and shepherding Catholics globally. Such a tour could help foster dialogue around faith, truth, beauty, history."

The tour would be a tremendous endeavor, but I was so inspired by the Pope's bold new leadership that I aimed high. My pitch was to help the Vatican take the "embarrassment" out what is truly an embarrassment of riches in their centuries-old collections. Proceeds from the tour could leverage these holdings that are worth billions of dollars, in order to help advance their mission of ministering to the less fortunate.

Meetings in Rome with Christie's colleagues followed. The Vatican Museum was interested, but not the Library. A second visit, in which we proposed a concrete business plan, raised our hopes. Weeks later came the disappointing news that the Museum would prefer to work with peer institutions, such as the Metropolitan Museum of Art.

In the course of those conversations, however, a senior advisor to Pope Francis's children's charity, Scholas Occurrentes, had sought me out to explore the concept of a charity auction. The Vatican had accumulated a trove of gifts from around the world that he was hoping to inventory and selectively sell to benefit the charity. This led to another year of dialogue and a trip to Buenos Aires before both parties agreed to sit tight for the time being. We proposed an e-commerce solution given the volume and value of the potential lots for sale. The channels of communications remained open and one day – says the optimist in me – it could happen.

The Vatican outreach was a moonshot moment for me. I made the initial approach on my own initiative. As I got traction, I kept growing the number of Christie's people engaged with the project. As much as I have preached starting small and test-driving your CSR activities, you can also build your CSR currency by nurturing one BHAG (a Big Hairy Audacious Goal) that you might just keep to yourself at first, and then share more broadly at the right time.

Leaders inspire action, and even when those actions do not bear fruit, they are still worthwhile. The lesson I took with this Vatican experience is that purpose and intentions are everything. If you align yourself and your company with those who share your values, only good can come of it. So aim high. Dream of a BHAG. Even if you miss, as we did with the Vatican, your colleagues will take note of your vision, and because of your aligned purpose and intentions, the relationships you develop will endure.

7.2. Declare Your Values
Kofi Annan

When it comes to the problem of poverty, the United Nations has made tremendous progress in recent years by serving as a conduit between the business world and the global community. Starting in 2000, under the leadership of General Secretary Kofi Annan, the UN initiated its Global Compact and Millennium Development Goals to help eradicate poverty around the world. By 2015 global poverty had been cut in half, in large part due to China's economic rise and by globalization's economic inclusion effects.

As Annan pointed out, however, globalization is not sustainable if its benefits accrue only to corporate shareholders. He said, "We must ensure that the global market is embedded in broadly shared values and practices that reflect global social needs, and that all the world's people share the benefits of globalization."

Without these shared values, CSR compliance has little meaning. That's why the Ten Principles for Responsible Leadership within the UN Global Compact are so important. The principles are related to human rights, labor rights, the environment, and the problems of bribery and governmental corruption. They were drawn from other previously set standards, such as the Universal

Declaration of Human Rights, and they offer a universal code of behavior in which all stakeholders treat each other respect and dignity.

When the UN launched its 17 Sustainable Development Goals (SDGs) and 169 specific measurable targets for progress, it provided businesses and governments with an invaluable set of guidelines for working together. At the same time, it is easy to see how the SDGs can be exploited and used for greenwashing by companies without an authentic commitment to CSR. The companies can boast about their contributions to 4 or 5 the SDGs, while quietly allowing its operations to work against the other 12 or 13 goals. Without values and principles, CSR is always at risk of becoming window dressing.

As the world hurtles towards 9 billion people, the UN, World Economic Forum and other global institutions are grappling with the challenges such growth poses – from food to health, to education, to energy, water, and climate change – all of which have the greatest impact on people in the developing world. The gap between rich and poor a major threat to world stability.

At the same time, the world is also filled with opportunities. At the 2017 World Economic Forum in Davos, the Business and Sustainable Development Committee's review of four key economic sectors (food and agriculture, cities and mobility, energy and materials, and health and well-being) revealed opportunities for business revenues and savings that could be worth more than $12 trillion by 2030, or about 10% of forecasted GDP.[49]

Annan's optimistic view is that businesses and civil institutions together have the skills and resources necessary for a healthy global community with a sustainable future. That future depends upon a more humane economy, one that reflects the true cost of business beyond the price of labor and materials, including its impact on people, communities, and the planet. The short-term obsession with shareholder value and stock price results means that without a significant change in values – the internal consensus about what matters – companies are doomed to fail in their obligation of ensuring their long-term success and viability.

7.3. Rethink Your Culture
Yidan "Charles" Chen
Pony Ma

There is not that much of a cultural tradition of philanthropy in China, at least not in the modern form we recognize in the West. But there is a huge company in China that is helping change that.

Tencent, as mentioned in the previous chapter, is a social media company with one billion subscribers through its WeChat platform, which combines the functions of WhatsApp, Facebook, Instagram, Twitter, and Snapchat, which also linking to customer bank accounts. Through the WeChat app, customers no longer need to carry credit cards, metro cards or cash.

In 2008, an earthquake in Sichuan killed 69,000 people and left vast areas of the province in ruins. Tencent engaged its users to help organize relief efforts and deliver supplies and donations to the stricken areas. That proved to be a turning point in the company's philanthropic efforts. Co-founders Yidan "Charles" Chen and Pony Ma, asked themselves what more they could do.

Today, Tencent Charity, the company's mobile and desktop donation site, has 100 million users, who have donated the equivalent of $250 million, an average of $2.50, each. For charity walks, the number of steps walked can be recorded on a mobile device and automatically draw matching funds from participating businesses. Tencent's popular e-payment system allows small donations of under $1 to be made to 24,000 different causes around the world. Customers can even "donate" their voice, by reading stories for the blind that are used in audio books. This is all in addition to the highly successful 9/9 Tencent Charity Day launched in 2015 and mentioned previously.[50]

Tencent Charity is using technology to evolve old-school philanthropy concepts in ways that resonate with its users, which in turn is driving change among charities and other NGOs in China. Competition for funds on the Tencent Charity platform has led to improvements in practices and transparency among these organizations. Ma and Chen have also launched their own personal philanthropic efforts, donating hundreds of millions of yuan toward educational awards and endowments, which had previously been fairly rare practices among China's new ultra-rich.

The exciting thing about CSR is that it inevitably changes culture, and for the better. For me, Tencent is a reminder that CSR begins to go away when it becomes part of mainstream culture, instead of standing outside of it. Changing a culture is difficult. The job of CSR often involves confronting the "way things have always been done," and shifting it towards this new, higher purpose. As these new behavioral norms take hold, as they have in China with Tencent, it is easy to see how the possibilities for new growth rapidly expand.

7.4. Raise the Bar
Paul Polman

In December 2017, the consumer goods giant Unilever introduced Love Beauty and Planet, a line of hair care, styling and body-care products developed with sustainable ingredients and packaging. A great deal of innovation went into the launch. All the ingredients are 100% plant-based. The line's conditioners are formulated with a proprietary Fast-Rinse technology, designed to rinse out of hair in under 10 seconds, allowing for less water to be used in the shower. Labels on the products are designed to withstand showering, but come off with heat applied at recycling facilities.

Love Beauty and Planet was developed as a part of Unilever's Sustainable Living Plan – the company's blueprint for reducing its environmental impact and attracting younger consumers whose choices are motivated by sustainability. The plan was launched in 2010 as an effort to double sales while halving the environmental impact of its products, improving the nutritional quality of its food products, and engaging smaller distributors, farmers, and other vendors in the company's supply chain.

Unilever's CEO, Paul Polman, is an evangelist for sustainability who sets the tone for CSR efforts at Unilever. "The word 'over-ambitious' does not exist when you look at the challenges we have to solve," he said in an interview. "We have been extremely ambitious and this has moved us out of our comfort zone."

He challenges his peers in the business world to do the same and keep raising the bar for what is achievable. "I don't think our fiduciary duty is to put shareholders first," he has said. "I say the opposite. What we firmly believe is that if we focus our company on improving the lives of the world's citizens and come up with genuine sustainable solutions, we are more in sync with consumers and society and ultimately this will result in good shareholder returns. Why would you invest in a company which is out of sync with the needs of society, that does not take its social compliance in its supply chain seriously, that does not think about the costs of externalities, or of its negative impacts on society?"

To me, Polman is a rock star. He sees beyond quarterly earnings reports and the bottom line to a more aspirational and long-term destination – while still managing the short-term realities of business. He has been able to look up and forward as he leads, unlike so many CEOs who keep their eyes downward, quarter-by-quarter, for fear of tripping or straying off course.

"Good CEOs," he has said, "in the future need to feel at ease working with multi-stakeholder groups and know how to work with them and how to align them to move things forward. It is an enormous learning curve as no one has been trained for this. . . . you have to be careful that you do not get involved in a million things as the world has so many problems [you must] ensure that the issues you do take on link to your business model and that you stay focused."

In my experience, you know when you are in the presence of a visionary leader. It is palpable. Their evangelical grounding assures them and generally those around them of their higher purpose and destination. They inspire others to follow.

They are also comfortable with being alone out front most of the time – because leadership can be a lonely place. Polman has come under severe criticism in the financial world from those who see Unilever's CSR efforts as mere "feel-good" measures that damage profitability. Polman notes: " [With Unilever], the Sustainable Living Plan is our business model. So we spend an enormous amount of time explaining it to our investors. Does everyone get it in the [investment community]? No, and to expect it will ever happen is wishful thinking. But investors will increasingly value our business on the basis of what we are doing."

Polman's view is that it is necessary to take some heat today in order to secure Unilever's long-term sustainability. Leaders of this kind do not necessarily expect to reap the full benefits of their courageous efforts. As the old story goes, one should plant seeds knowing you may not live to long enough to enjoy the shade of the tree it will become. The lesson is to keep planting seeds, keep raising the bar. Leadership in the style of Paul Polman is its own reward.

7.5. Invest in People
Marjorie Yang

You may not know Marjorie Yang by name, but you very likely have worn her clothes. Yang is chairman of Hong Kong's Esquel Group, the global textile and apparel manufacturer that produces more than 110 million shirts every year for brands that include Gap, Nike, Patagonia, Ralph Lauren, Hugo Boss, and Tommy Hilfiger.

Esquel is a CSR leader in the textile industry, an industry with a poor reputation for worker conditions. When visiting its largest factory in Gaoming, China, you might think you have found a workers' utopia, with state-of-the-art technology, generous employee benefits, and on-site schools and health clinics. Energy and water consumption has been cut in half in the past decade. Automation has improved efficiency and product quality, allowing factories to pay higher wages than other nearby clothing makers.

I first met Marjorie her when I was launching the Green Auction at Christie's and she was a member of Christie's Asia Advisory Board, along with other notables such as Baroness Lydia Dunn, David Li, and Robert Tsao. From the start, she happily supported me and our untested concept.

Yang's determination and personal commitment to enlightened business practices are nothing short of evangelical. In 2014 along with her dynamo daughter Dee Poon she launched the Integral Conversation, extending Esquel's influence far beyond the echelons of the textile and apparel industries. This annual event convenes thought leaders and experts from diverse fields to bring together their insights and perspectives on a range of topics in relation to sustainability including manufacturing, building and construction, products and technologies, culture and tourism, and more. It was at the 2015 event that I had the good fortune of moderating a fireside chat with Susan and David Rockefeller on the state of philanthropy. Our dialogue along with 300 other guests and media allowed us to reflect on the future of sustainable development and how we might achieve economic progress in harmony with the environment and society.

Under Yang's leadership, the Esquel CSR department occupies a strategically important position, responsible for advising the CEO and other senior managers on risks inside the business related to the lack of close adherence to international labor standards. The approach is very much attuned to the bullseye of stakeholders: employees, customers, and planet, as the CSR department engages with customer concerns over environmental impacts and health and safety in the workplace. Yang and her colleagues require their suppliers to share a commitment to operate in a legal and ethical manner. Esquel's code of conduct covers the behavior of its suppliers as well as its proprietary facilities.

As noted on Esquel's homepage, "At Esquel, we do not see CSR as a defensive strategy, in reaction to international criticism of working conditions in regions with low cost labor. Rather, we would like to set a positive example and prove that a company can be both profitable and committed to sustainability and worker welfare. On top of internal reviews and hosting numerous customer audits, ongoing training is conducted for Esquel employees on labor, environment, health, and safety standards."

Yang inherited Esquel as a family business and has overseen its growth (doubling its revenue to $1.4 billion between 2008 and 2014) as well as its development as a CSR leader. "Our industry is facing a lot of pressure, and many manufacturers think that sustainability is just about image," Yang once said at a textile conference. "But my father, who founded the company, taught me that when you run a company you have to take responsibility for the environment and society."

7.6. Break Boundaries
Oprah Winfrey
Persevere

Few people have overcome childhood adversity more magnificently than Oprah Winfrey. Born in rural Mississippi to a single mother, she was raped at the age of nine by a teenage cousin and suffered further sexual abuse from an uncle and a family friend. She was moved from her grandmother's Mississippi home to a Milwaukee boarding home to live with her mother, and then to Nashville with her father.

A scholarship to Tennessee State University led to a career in local broadcast news, which in turn led to her syndicated talk show, running from 1986 to 2011. The show made her one of the nation's most influential people, and, with a net worth estimated at $3 billion, the wealthiest African-American in history.

Winfrey is an example of someone who, having had terrible adversity thrust upon her, has been strengthened by those experiences and persevered. She took a white, male dominated talk-show format to unprecedented levels of critical and financial success; she countered the challenge that print publishing was dying with the immense success of her Book Club; she is the most influential investor and spokesperson for Weight Watchers life affirming products and services.

Once proclaimed the "Queen of All Media", Winfrey has managed to be a force in business, media, philanthropy, politics, and an evangelist for good. Committed to storytelling about the downtrodden and disenfranchised, the Emmy winner and Oscar honoree has long been touted as a potential candidate for public office, including the presidency.

She has given away an estimated $400 million through her Oprah Winfrey Charitable Foundation, and has funded mostly educational causes, such as the Oprah Winfrey Leadership Academy for girls in South Africa. Throughout her personal and professional activities, Oprah has never stopped educating and engaging people in a pursuit of a better world, constantly illuminating, clarifying, and ultimately elevating all of us through her work.

Every step in her career has been led by disruption followed by a sublime balancing of commercial sensibilities with higher purpose. Almost like a human mobius strip, one aspect blends effortlessly into the other. Having been cared for very poorly as a child, everything she does illustrates her leadership position in the Caring Economy.

7.7. Share What You Know: Go Open Source
Elon Musk

One of the things I have extolled in this book is how CSR is an information-sharing community. We are all in this together. If you are not drawing on the experience and advice of your peers, you are really missing out.

The fact is that sharing and transparency are gaining ground in business in general, and the future will continue to see growth in the practice. One of the more notable examples is how Tesla chairman Elon Musk decided to put all of the company's 1,400 patents in the public domain, royalty-free. The company's stock boomed with the announcement, suggesting that, when it comes to intellectual property, it is often the giving hand that gets

There is a degree of self-interest in Tesla's choice to share. By making its own patents public, it raises the odds that Tesla's systems will become the industry standard, which is good for Tesla. However, the industry as a whole will gain when certain manufacturing choices are standardized, for instance, when charging stations all have the same type of plug.

The larger point is that Musk and the Tesla brain trust do not consider other electric carmakers to be competitors. You rarely hear them speaking ill of rival electric car models. That's because Musk's evangelism concerns the virtues of electric power over the combustion engine, not Tesla over other manufacturers.

"Our goal when we created Tesla a decade ago was the same as it is today," Musk has said, "to accelerate the advent of sustainable transport by bringing compelling mass market electric cars to market as soon as possible." Hoarding technology does not advance that mission. Sharing it does.

Musk caused a dustup in the business press in 2018 by stating in a quarterly earnings call that when expanding Tesla's costly network of charging stations across the U.S., he would prefer if the stations were available to charge all kinds of electric cars, not just Tesla's. A stock analyst questioned whether that was wise. After all, as the leading electric car manufacturer, having a proprietary network of charging stations would serve as a protective "moat" against competing electric car brands.

"First of all, I think moats are lame," Musk replied. "It's nice sort of quaint in a vestigial way. If your only defense against invading armies is a moat, you will not last long. What matters is the pace of innovation. That is the fundamental determinant of competitiveness."

Musk is probably the top corporate evangelist in the U.S. today, with Tesla and with all his other ongoing projects, including space rockets, a transportation tunneling company and massive battery farms that store wind energy. His companies are by no means perfect in terms of sustainability, and have faced more than their share of CSR challenges. It is Musk's tendency towards openness and transparency that has earned him the benefit of the doubt many times over.

Maintaining a general bias toward sharing and open-source solutions is critical to long-term success in CSR. Technology is pushing us relentlessly toward a more collaborative and transparent world. If you deny it, you're swimming against a powerful current. With CSR, it is actually just as easy to be inclusive as exclusive, and how you avail yourself to collaborators will be a key variable in your impact. A lack of transparency and inclusiveness is likely to trip you up in whatever you try to achieve. Closing off access to discussion deprives your ideas of the oxygen necessary to breathe and grow.

7.8. Partner for Progress
Jamie Dimon

"I've never had this conflict between shareholders and corporate social responsibility," says Jamie Dimon, CEO of JPMorgan Chase. His firm has partnered with the city of Detroit, where Chase Bank has a significant market share, to help bring back jobs and revitalize the city. JPMorgan Chase has worked with city officials in areas where the company is uniquely able to help – donating its own data tools and resources so it could help the city make smart investments and planning decisions. This is the future of corporate purpose: becoming a true partner for change.

Through New Skills at Work, a five-year $250 million global initiative, JPMorgan Chase is leveraging its unique set of resources, expertise, and global reach to support skills training for adults. A second program, New Skills For Youth, addresses the specific problem of youth unemployment with $75 million for expanded skills education.

Dimon advises leaders to invest in overlooked communities and develop practical solutions to revitalize the disenfranchised communities. He has evangelized throughout his tenure for corporations to look beyond simply giving financial support, to donating their time, talent, and resources to addressing larger challenges including economic gaps, veterans affairs, and rebuilding cities such as Detroit.

"We've done a terrible job – 'we' being collectively the leadership of America – in trying to make sure all of our citizens don't fall behind," Dimon said at the 2017 at the 2017 Fortune CEO Initiative. Dimon points out the irony that employers are having trouble filling jobs in skilled labor and professional positions, while poverty and unemployment remain high all over the world. "We could do a far better job in education, re-location, and income assistance that leads to jobs. There are five million open jobs in America, and a lot of these jobs [in] aviation, automotive, nursing, robotics, machine learning coding, are well paying."

A CSR program that is limited to philanthropic giving misses out on truly participating in the Caring Economy. The challenge of building partnerships, however, is that you must choose partners carefully, because it is impossible to make a positive contribution to a non-profit or government that is mismanaged. Dimon said that his firm will not work with cities that are unable to prove they will be reliable, effective partners. "It's a 'sine qua non' lesson. If you go into any place and they just say, 'Give us the money, we'll take it from there' don't do it. They've got to agree up front to do some very basic things so you know you can work with them. It's a collaboration."

7.9. Imagine New Paradigms
Blockchain

I remember Time magazine's issue of January 3, 1983, when the cover of its annual Man of the Year issue (Time had not yet changed it to "Person of the Year") was devoted to a picture of a machine. Breaking with decades of naming each year's most influential person in the news, the magazine named the personal computer as its first-ever Machine of the Year. In terms of impact and influence, the personal computer that year outdistanced all the other human contenders.

I am reminded of that cover in as we contemplate the dawn of the Caring Economy. I say this because in my mind, it is conceivable that technology could outperform humans in creating a more inclusive and compassionate world. The zenith of a Caring Economy might be achieved not by humans but by new technologies doing work once reserved for humans.

Consider blockchain technology, for example. The most famous applications of blockchain technology is its use in cryptocurrencies like Bitcoin, but blockchain's power beyond money is its unique ability to provide transparency in all kinds of transactions without relying on corruptible human systems of trust. Blockchains may soon provide a new paradigm for trust, which is now in such short supply within human-dependent business and governmental systems.

Blockchains are essentially automatically notarized ledgers that are 100% transparent and unalterable. They alleviate the need for authentication by middlemen and regulatory agencies. As such, blockchains may vastly reduce fraud, system risk, legal fees, and other costs associated with any number of transactions.

According to Alex Tapscott's book, "Blockchain Revolution," the technology is poised to revolutionize the world, describing it as: "a truly open, distributed, global platform that will fundamentally change what we can achieve online, how we do it, and who can participate."

Fundamental CSR values such as transparency, authenticity, and security are all automated through blockchains. For instance, Blockchain may soon document the full chain of custody from the product's creation – including materials used, workforce that created it, and the environmental impact of its lifespan. Transparency is a guarantor of accountability and, in turn, responsibility. By offering complete traceability of records, blockchains might provide consumers with the assurance that products such as diamonds, wood, or seafood do not come from contraband sources, Blockchain may make it impossible for irresponsible providers to operate.

With its permanent, distributed record of transactions, blockchain can cut corruption and waste. It is estimated that 30% of global aid never reaches its rightful destination.[51] The Government of India, for instance, is using blockchain to fight the problem of land fraud.[52] Various agencies are already using the technology for international aid payments and helping refugees. Blockchain might help the 1.1 billion people worldwide who do not have an officially-recorded identity gain access to bank accounts, loans, and government services.[53]

"Unlike any technology before it, blockchain is transforming the way like-minded organizations come together and enabling a new level of trust based on a single view of the truth," said Marie Wieck, general manager of IBM Blockchain.[54] "Our work with organizations across the food ecosystem, as well as IBM's new platform, will further unleash the vast potential of this exciting technology, making it faster for organizations of all sizes and in all industries to move from concept to production to improve the way business gets done."

By bringing greater transparency to industries and consumers, blockchain may also remove the need for many of the functions CSR programs have typically provided, such as monitoring and reporting on inputs and logistics. Information is power and blockchain technology could spread that power to a more rational, factual, and just place. By making many finance, legal, Human Resources, and CSR-related jobs and roles obsolete, blockchain technology could amplify the positive impact of business, for all stakeholders, not simply shareholders.

7.10. See Your Evangelist in the Mirror

In the coming decade, the spread of CSR will rely more and more on evangelists within every organization promoting CSR's continually expanding domain. Seeing yourself as an evangelist means becoming a reliable messenger, a source of knowledge and wisdom about this new way of doing business.

The trends are your friends. Keep pushing the boundaries of where you see opportunities for change and progress, because if this book has demonstrated anything, it is shown that the wind is at your back. The news you bring to your organization will direct the collective CSR push that will make all the difference in sustainability – for your personal career and for the organization's collective results.

Never forget that you are lending your time, talent, and your company's treasure to one of the most powerful and meaningful movements in economic history. To quote Churchill, "We make a living by what we get. We make a life by what we give." Your role may call on you to stretch beyond your comfort zone at times. It is at those times when you must remind yourself of the CSR cause and your sense of mission and purpose. If you do not consider yourself a pushy person in the moment when something or someone requires a shove, try to think holistically, collaborate energetically and mind your values. Keep your CSR values clear in your mind and in your heart, then when there are times to make difficult choices, you can always trust your gut.

If you pursue CSR with authenticity, with your heart and soul engaged, you will win in the long run, because you are moving with the tide of history. Perhaps your actual impact is less than optimal. And you may not get credit for the difference that you make. Long after you are gone from your current role, your work will continue to impact others in ways that can never be known to you.

The important thing, I believe, is to maintain focus on moving forward. No matter the outcome, no matter who gets the credit, never forget that you are part of an ongoing revolution that is changing the world. Momentum is your friend with CSR. Even if a project fails to make a meaningful contribution to your company's aims and goals, the experience of falling short will add to your personal and professional growth. You will be that much stronger when facing your next challenge. The progress you make each day will never be wasted, no matter how small.

Here is a very personal example of what I mean. Back in 2006, when I was putting together the first Green Auction at

Christie's, I knew that my decades-long friendship with environmentalist Susan Rockefeller would contribute to the project's success. The Rockefeller Family is among the world's greatest art collecting families, and through its foundations, it is also deeply involved in environmental advocacy. Susan and David Rockefeller, in particular, are true global leaders in sustainability.

With Susan's help, and the help of others Susan was able to bring on board, The Green Auction was a tremendous success. It raised $5 million for global environmental organizations, and their ongoing efforts to protect the planet. One of the four beneficiaries of the Green Auction was Oceana (the world's leading proponent of healthy oceans), where Susan is a trustee.

Following the Green Auction, Christie's continued to collaborate with the Rockefellers on Oceana and various initiatives, largely through our CSR efforts. Christie's charity auctioneers and venues were put to good use for Rockefeller-supported organizations (including Oceana, the Asian Cultural Council, Sailors for the Sea). Christie's also helped promote events for organizations that mattered to the family including MoMA and the Stone Barns Center for Food and Agriculture, a unique sustainable farming project near the Rockefeller Estate in Westchester County, New York.

In 2010, David Rockefeller, the last surviving grandson of John D. Rockefeller, made it known that the family's vast art holdings would be part of an estate sale auction, with all the proceeds to be devoted to the Rockefeller family's philanthropic pursuits. Christie's and Sotheby's submitted proposals to be the auction house of choice for the massive undertaking of running the estate sale, and Christie's was selected.

"Those years of working together on Oceana auctions built trusting human relationships," David told me. "The core of our decision was a business judgment, but the other important elements of trust, character, and style enabled the executors of my dad's estate to comfortably make Christie's our choice."

In May 2018, Christie's auction of the Peggy and David Rockefeller Collection, raised $832 million to benefit a dozen non-profit organizations, including the Museum of Modern Art, Rockefeller University, Harvard University, the Council on Foreign Relations, and the Stone Barns Center (where I am proud to be a member of the development committee).

When the Rockefeller estate auction was announced, I had been gone from Christie's for two years and had launched my own advisory firm, Philanthropic Impact (∏). I was delighted that Christie's had been chosen for such an important, once-in-a-lifetime endeavor. I hoped, as David had suggested, that years of charity auctions and our CSR program had helped Christie's and the Rockefellers grow familiar with their shared sets of values and tastes, making the choice of auction house a natural fit.

On the other hand, the CSR work we did with the Rockefeller family and many others speaks for itself. Through Art + Soul, Christie's employees and clients joined together to make an incalculable impact on our communities and the planet. Thousands of charities and their patrons are supported every year by the army of charity auctioneers organized under the umbrella of Art + Soul. As a result of all these activities, thousands of Christie's employees, not-for-profit staff members, and young students around the globe connected in museums, schools, and parks to help steward culture and nature in their hometowns.

I left Christie's in 2015 with a feeling that my work was incomplete, that the company's culture had not really been transformed, as I had hoped when I first took on the CSR role. I think it is common in management positions to wonder in retrospect if you could have made a bigger difference, but I suspect it is a particular kind of occupational hazard with CSR. We do this work because we care so much, and emotional attachments to results naturally follow. This is where thousands of years of Eastern philosophy can be of some help. Try to embrace how the way of true wisdom is to do the right thing without expectations. If you can learn to take the proverbial "right action without desire," you will find that choices are easier to make. They will also be much, much easier to live with.

In that spirit, I continue my connection with Christie's. I helped Christie's seek Chinese sponsors for the China tour of the Rockefeller Collection in advance of the estate sale. Last year I taught a master's degree program on non-profit arts management at Christie's Education. These are things worth doing, with little calculation on my part as to the result. It is partly what I mean by pursuing CSR with authenticity. My heart and soul are engaged, and that is enough.

It all matters in the Caring Economy.

So today, I believe that it all matters with CSR, event if not as much to some people as to others. But all CSR efforts create a better world and strengthen your business to remain competitive. We did make a difference in our community with Art + Soul. As Christie's CSR evangelist, at every turn I had to engage colleagues, partners, media, and world class collectors to the best of my ability with limited resources. The work was sweetened by the friendships we created or deepened with NGOs and colleagues.

As you evangelize for your CSR, you need to do so with similar authenticity and commitment to relationships rather than transactions. It will make all the difference and you will know it, even if you are not there to witness your long-term impact. At the dawn of the Caring Economy, you can help your company win.

Doing the right thing, by the way, means doing it before it is expected of you. It also means doing it because it means something to you, not because you think someone is watching. If your initiative does not tie into your brand story, you are potentially opening yourself up to a world of scrutiny and backlash.

The forces of opposition remain quite formidable. Most people tend to acquiesce to the way things are, and there are many millions (as evidenced by the 2016 election) who see change and progress as a palpable threat. In his book "Utopia Drive: A Road Trip Through America's Most Radical Idea," Erik Reece writes how U.S. financial and industrial power extinguished many of the utopian ideals of the late 19th century and "ultimately created an American consumer culture so unsustainable and so devoid of idealism that we now stand on the verge of both environmental calamity and an intractable federal plutocracy – a government given over to the rich by a bewildered, defeatist populace."

So we must persevere in the fact of that gloomy assessment and others. But we should also take comfort in the fact that unsustainability is writing its own death warrant every day. The utopian for CSR is a point of arrival where a company's CSR unit closes because the company is so evolved that CSR is no longer necessary as a distinct function. The end of CSR will not mean the end of your role in the cause. It will mean the elevation of everyone who understands that social responsibility is the key to the future of all sustainable businesses.

The next time a board member or company executive suggests a new CSR initiative, keep in mind that the downside potential of not doing the right thing is still big, but the upside is disappearing. Being responsible is no longer an option. Some brands investing heavily in these areas fail to understand that the morally correct choice is now a standard expectation from young people – and every day thousands of babies are born who will only know that world.

There is no constant in this new world except change. Through the changes to come, only values will endure. That is the closest thing to a crystal ball I can offer. Your values as expressed through your CSR will prepare you and your company to flourish in a Caring Economy.

Vatican Letters

From: TUsnik@christies.com
To: direttore.musei@scv.va; Jean-Louis.Brugu?s@scv.va
CC: aniccolini@camugliano.com
Subject: The Vatican Highlights Global Tour 2015-2016
Date: Wed, 18 Dec 2013 21:46:45 +0000

Dear Monsignor Bruguès and Director Paolucci,

As a Catholic inspired by Pope Francis and as head of Corporate Social Responsibility at Christie's, I'm writing to engage you in a conversation about creating a global tour of highlights from the Vatican Library and Vatican Museums to support the mission and vision of Pope Francis and the Catholic Church. Such a tour to cathedrals in select capitals of the world could bring Catholics and non-Catholics alike together in an dialogue about faith, beauty, history, truth and our common humanity.

With nearly 250 years of experience, Christie's is uniquely positioned to help convene and connect individuals and institutions at the highest levels, from corporate sponsors of the tour, to curators and historians of art and culture to the clergy. If one considers the Vatican as having an embarrassment of riches that a finite universe ever gets to see in person, a global tour could in effect take out the 'embarrassment' and share the truth, history and beauty of such works and faith with a truly global audience.

This is a very brief and bold outline, but I am hopeful that it might lead to at least a phone conversation or a meeting in Rome in 2014 when it suits you. I wish you the very best and thank you for your consideration.

Sincerely,

Toby Usnik Chief Corporate Social Responsibility Officer & International Director

---

CHRISTIE'S

20 Rockefeller Plaza New York, NY 10020 **Tel:** +1 (212) 636
2680 **Mobile:** +1 (917) 751 7778
Email: tusnik@christies.com

- **What:** Global tour of Selections from the Vatican Library and
Vatican Museums
- **Who:** Vatican (Pope and curators), Christie's (covening and
connecting; sourcing funders), Corporate/Individual Sponsors who
underwrite in each city.
- **When:** 2015-2016
- **Where:** Cathedrals and National Libraries (maybe some
museums) across multiple cities that are high priority for the Vatican
and Christie's, including Mexico City, Sao Paulo, Los Angeles,
Singapore, Beijing, CIS states and Qatar.
- **Why:** Chrisitie's is uniquely positioned to convene and connect
influencers across the art market at the highest levels to advance a
noble mission – sharing one of the greatest collections that will never
come to market with the largest possible population. It would be
consistent with Pope Francis's democratization of the church and
shepherding Catholics globally. Such a tour could help foster
dialouge around faith, truth, beauty, history.

http://en.wikipedia.org/wiki/Vatican_Library
http://mv.vatican.va/3_EN/pages/MV_Home.html

- -

Visit www.christies.com to explore special multi-media sale
promotions, browse our illustrated catalogues and leave absentee
bids through LotFinder(R), Christie's online search engine, and
register for Internet bidding with Christie's Live(TM).

S.E. Mons. Jean-Louis Brugès, O.P.
Archivista e Bibliotecario di S.R.C.

Prot. 2014/0062/B-B997
Vatican City, 9 January 2014

Dear Mr. Usnik,

I received your letter of December 18th requesting a meeting or a phone conversation about a possible global tour project in 2015-2016.

It could be an interesting occasion for a meeting the next time you are coming to Rome. If you let me know a date in advance, I could check the possibility of such an encounter.

Sincerely Yours in Christ,

+ Jean-Louis Brugès

✠ Jean-Louis Brugès, O.P.
Archivist and Librarian H.R.C.

Mr. Toby Usnik
Chief Social Responsibility Officer
International Director
CHRISTIE'S
20 Rockefeller Plaza
New York, NY 10020
USA

160

10 March 2014

His Excellency Jean-Louis Bruguès, O.P.
Cortile Del Belvedere
00120 Città del Vaticano

Your Excellency O.P.,

On behalf of my colleagues, Jussi Pylkkanen and Alessandra Niccolini, I am writing to thank you for accommodating our 26 February meeting in Vatican City with yourself, Monsignore Paolo Nicolini of the Musei Vaticani, and Monsignore Cesare Pasini, Dottor Ambrogio M. Piazzoni, and Dottoressa Amalia D'Alascio of the Biblioteca Apostolica Vaticana. It was an honor for us to share our passion for culture and corporate social responsibility and to learn that you also share a belief in the power of art to transcend borders and politics and to comfort, inspire and unite people.

As promised, we have summarized on the following pages the main points we heard in our discussion and have also suggested some possible next steps. Please let us know if anything was lost or misstated due to translation. From our perspective, the desire to collaborate in a non-commercial, humanistic initiative is genuine and achievable. Furthermore, such an initiative would be carried out in collaboration with you with Christie's global network of offices and the expertise of Christie's professionals.

Given that our conversation touched upon China, Latin America and other parts of the world, we would like to ask for additional guidance from you on which two to three countries we might begin with as we outline a more detailed, formal proposal for an exhibition? Additionally, given the depth and breadth of the Vatican's holdings, we would welcome additional direction from you on items to include in a potential joint initiative. We have taken the liberty of providing some examples of works -- religious and secular -- that we believe would be compelling for a generic visitor. However, with a more complete inventory of your holdings, we can better tailor an exhibition to the selected community. Through dialogue with Vatican curators and librarians, we would refine the list significantly.

I will phone your office next week to confirm receipt of this letter and to answer any questions you may have. I am also including the extra two Christie's logo bags I promised you. Thank you for your time and consideration.

Sincerely,

Toby Usnik
Chief Corporate Social Responsibility Officer

CC: Monsignore Paolo Nicolini, Delegato amministrativo-gestionale, Musei Vaticani
        Monsignore Cesare Pasini, Prefetto, Biblioteca Apostolica Vaticana
        Dottor Ambrogio M. Piazzoni, Vice Prefetto, Biblioteca Apostolica Vaticana
        Dottoressa Amalia D'Alascio, Responsabile Ufficio Mostre, Biblioteca Apostolica Vaticana
        Jussi Pylkkanen, President & Chairman, Christies Europe, Middle East, Russia & India
        Alessandra Niccolini, International Advisor, Christie's

Summary of Main Points

- All agree that no works are for sale and that our collective aim would be to share highlights of the Vatican Collections with a broader audience to foster dialogue about art, faith, beauty and humanity. The collaboration would be open to all cultures, respectful in its tone, and educational, not commercial.

- We need to confirm countries where the Vatican and Christie's would be keen to hold a major exhibition. Then we can carefully design the exhibition to suit the culture and heritage of the country in question. In our meeting, your members suggested Mainland China or Latin America as potential venues.

- Christie's acknowledges that the Vatican is a complex entity – a state, an institution, and a spiritual center – and requires diplomacy in its collaborations. Christie's has worked previously with the Vatican and countless governments, royal families, corporations, museums, libraries and charities, and we believe Christie's is an ideal partner for a Vatican exhibition.

- We would commit to a collaboration that is transparent and logical so as to avoid any conflict of interest or even the appearance of a conflict of interest, consistent with Christie's Corporate Social Responsibility mission outlined in the attached document.

- All agree that we are in a historic moment in which economic crises, politics and cultural and societal shifts are making art an important shared language. Christie's noted that this is particularly the case in many of the emerging economies where we have been building cultural bridges over the past five years (e.g., Russia, the Middle East, China, India and Latin America).

- Concurrently, all agreed that art is often viewed as a great subject but that it is increasingly seen as the domain of the rich.

- All agree that any exhibition would be of the highest quality in terms of the objects and the curatorial and promotional expertise used to present them.

- Conservation of the Vatican Collections is costly. Christie's is uniquely positioned to help introduce members of the cultural community to the Vatican to help in its conservation, promotion and acquisition efforts.

- For any exhibition, Christie's would use its 250-years' experience and expertise to manage the following, among other elements: funding, logistics and shipping, insurance, event production, catalogue production, marketing and public relations, security, staffing and legal issues.

- If the Vatican wishes to raise funds for charity through an exhibition, Christie's has expertise in facilitating it, as noted in the materials shared during our meeting. In 2013 and outside of our own sale rooms, Christie's charity auctioneers volunteered personal time and raised over $65 million for more than 150 charities globally.

Next Steps / Ways to Collaborate

- We would like to agree to key three 'next steps'. We would suggest: 1) The Vatican confirms which city (cities) it would like to begin with; 2) The Vatican recommends preferred resource materials on its holdings and/or provide a comprehensive inventory of holdings to be reviewed by Christie's specialists as they create a formal tour proposal; 3) We agree on dates and attendees for next meeting.

- With a target audience identified and comprehensive inventory of works, Christie's can develop the exhibition proposal in approximately 6 weeks. Such a plan would include budgets, timelines, audiences, marketing and public relations plans, event schedules and a list of targeted sponsors.

- Finally, in addition to exhibitions and tours, Christie's stands at the ready to assist Vatican staff with further development/fundraising exercises, reconnaissance on artworks that they are seeking but unable to find or afford to acquire, and convening/connecting with cultural patrons at the highest levels. Christie's Education, Christie's International Real Estate, Christie's Estates/Appraisals/Valuations (EAV), and Christie's Fine Arts Storage also remain at the Vatican's avail for possible collaborations.

2

162

Works and Categories for Discussion

Rare Books, Manuscripts and Documents

* A letter dated 1246 from Grand Khan Guyuk, Genghis Khan's grandson to Pope Innocent IV
* Galileo's signature "admitting" at the conclusion of the pope's Inquisition Tribunal in 1633 that he had committed heresy by stating that Earth revolved around the sun and not the other way around
* The 1521 bull of excommunication of Martin Luther
* The letter that Mary, Queen of Scots wrote while awaiting execution
* Documents taken by Napoleon and later returned to the Vatican
* The letter from English nobles to the pope in 1530 demanding that Henry VIII be allowed to divorce Catherine of Aragon--which the pope denied, leading to the formation of the Church of England
* The papal bull that divided up the New World between Spain and Portugal at the time when Columbus came back from the Americas in 1493
* The short note Marie Antoinette wrote from prison just before she was executed
* Documents from the 1308 trials of the Knight Templars before Pope Clement V disbanded them
* The letter from Michelangelo complaining about delays in his work on the dome of St. Peter's Basilica
* Bodmer Papyrus XIV-XV
* Documents related to Copernican theory of the universe
* A letter from the Ojibwe tribe of Native Americans from Grassy Lake, Ontario written on birch bark in 1887 to Pope Leo XIII
* Letter from Chinese empress Helena pledging her allegiance to Catholicism

Ethnographic Materials & Antiquities

* Bundu helmet mask of the Sande female society
* Sculpture of Quetzalcóatl (Aztec), Pre-Colombian Mexican divinity
* Sculpture of Tu, main divinity of the pantheon of Mangareva Island
* Statue of Apollo del Belvedere
* Selection of Gregorian Etruscan Museum Greek ceramics, vases, jewelry, bronzes
* The Prima Porta Augustus, Doryphorus
* Torso of the Egyptian Pharaoh Nectanebo I (380-362 B.C.)
* Red-Figured Hydria, Attic, C. 510 B.C., attributed to Euthymides
* Burial stele for a young man, from Ancient Sculpture Collection
* One of Niobe's Daughters, from Ancient Sculpture Collection
* Vestment Set with the Arms of Clement IX and Renato Borromeo, Count of Arona: Stole, maniple, chalice veil and burse.
* Selection of Galeria Lapidaria objects, including tablets and inscriptions
* *Madurn Italy*, Luc Holste, 1632-1633, map
* *Two Greyhounds Playing*, Roman artist, 1st-2nd century

Old Master Works

* *Portrait of St. Jerome in the Wilderness*, Leonardo da Vinci, c. 1482
* *Deposition from the Cross*, Caravaggio, c. 1600-1604
* Any works by painters Fra Angelico, Giotto, Raphael, Nicolas Poussin and Titian
* *Mary Magdalene*, Guercino (Giovanni Francesco Barbieri), 1622

3

Modern & Contemporary Works

* *The Church at Carrieres-Saint-Denis*, Andre Derain, 1909
* *Third Allegory*, Ben Shahn, 1969
* *The Tree of Life (L'Arbre de Vie)*, Henri Matisse, 1949
* *The Daughters of Lot*, Carlo Carra, 1940
* *The Holy Tunic*, Fernand Leger after 1945, stained glass window
* Works from *Creation, Uncreation, Recreation* from the 2013 Vatican Pavilion, Venice Biennale
    o "Creation" – Studio Azzurro's new media collective exploring the links between information technology and art, including interactive video installation.
    o "Un-Creation" – Koudelka's 18 photographs taken between 1986 and 2012 whose works deals with social and political issues.
    o "Re-Creation" – Carroll's installation of four wall paintings and a floor piece, as well as lighting, using recycled materials and is abstract in nature.

Other

* One of the carriages or motorcars of Popes and Cardinals, perhaps one of the first cars used by Popes.

# # #

4

GOVERNATORATO
DIREZIONE DEI MUSEI

CITTÀ DEL VATICANO.   I 6 SET. 2014

14717/2014-18

Dear Mr. Usnik,

   With reference to previous conversations and correspondence and after careful analysis, we are pleased to inform you that your project is of great interest to the Vatican Museums.
However, considering all the activities that have already been planned, we are unable to address any new proposals at this particular time.
We will contact you once we have reviewed our programming for the year 2015.
Thank you for your interest and patience.

   Kind regards,

Msgr. Paolo Nicolini

<u>tusnik@christies.com</u>

Mr. Toby Usnik
Chief Corporate Social Responsibility Officer
CHRISTIE'S
20 Rockefeller Plaza
New York, NY 10020
USA

MUSEI VATICANI, V- 00120 Città del Vaticano - Tel. (+39) 06 698.83332; Fax (+39) 06 698.85061

Acknowledgments

I would like to express my gratitude to the many people who helped make this book possible, past and present; to all those who provided support, talked things over, read, wrote, offered comments, allowed me to quote their remarks and assisted in the editing, proofreading and design. In particular, I would like to thank Noel Weyrich for coaching me over these past two years of writing, always making the effort more fun and the result even stronger.

The foundation of this book began early with my family and the values they instilled in me, particularly my mother, Sally. This was further refined by the faculty and staff of Hampden-Sydney College, with its 240-year mission to "form good men and good citizens since 1776." My belief in the importance of community – building, advancing and protecting it – was then set in stone by my chosen family of friends when I came to New York City in 1988, particularly Greg Henniger, Mitchell Klein, David Liu, Ed Bergman and Susan Cohn Rockefeller.

To my American Express colleagues, particularly Elisabeth Coleman, Nancy Muller, Mike O'Neill and Melissa Abernathy, who helped me hone my professional skills at one of the world's leading service brands. To my New York Times Company colleagues, including Catherine Mathis, Trish McSweeney, Ethan Riegelhaupt, Janet Robinson and Arthur Sulzberger, Jr., who showed me that business can and must enhance society. To my Christie's colleagues who took a leap of faith with me in adding a bit of soul to the otherwise transactionally-obsessed art market, particularly Katelyn Norris, Lydia Fenet, Cathy Elkies, Ed Dolman, Mariangela Renshaw, Marc Porter, Stephen Lash and Karen Gray. And to my ArtsCom colleagues, particularly Mary Trudell, who embody the spirit of collaboration as we engage the next generation of culture-seekers.

I also wish to acknowledge my fellow CSR practitioners and business leaders who have inspired me as I launched my advisory Philanthropic Impact (π), including Francois-Henri Pinault, Richard and Nancy Liu, Lamberto Andreotti, Pino Brusone, William Floyd,

Julie Gilhart, Jennifer Schwab, Andrew Zobler, Andrea Sullivan, Paul Polman, Sue Allchurch, Pony Ma, Denise Simon, Gwen Green, Jamie Dimon and Sally Susman, among others. And I wish to thank civil society leaders – particularly Susan and David Rockefeller – and Paul and Moying Marcus, Darren Walker, Melissa Ong, Horacio Srur, Gary Wasserman, Cui Qiao, Iliana van Meeteren, Emily Rafferty and Michael Bloomberg for their ongoing inspiration.

Last and not least, I thank my husband Harlan Bratcher for sharing life with me.

Toby Usnik
August 2018
New York City

Endnotes

[1] https://www.christies.com/about-us/corporate-social-responsibility/awards-and-recognitions/

[2] http://www.pewresearch.org/topics/millennials/

[3] https://papers.ssrn.com/sol3/papers.cfm?abstract_id=2575912

[4] https://www.blackrock.com/corporate/investor-relations/larry-fink-ceo-letter

[5] http://mallenbaker.net/article/clear-reflection/how-tim-cook-brought-corporate-social-responsibility-to-apple

[6] http://mallenbaker.net/article/clear-reflection/how-tim-cook-brought-corporate-social-responsibility-to-apple

[7] https://www.unicefusa.org/press/releases/gucci-launches-new-global-campaign-girls'-and-women's-empowerment/8212

[8] https://corporate.target.com/corporate-responsibility/goals-reporting

[9] https://www.kornferry.com/press/korn-ferry-hay-group-global-study-finds-employee-engagement-at-critically-low-levels/

[10] http://www.gesustainability.com/building-things-that-matter/supply-chain/supplier-expectations/

[11] http://www.gesustainability.com/how-ge-works/

[12] https://www.wespire.com/press-room/survey-finds-57-percent-of-workers-want-employers-to-increase-employee-engagement/

[13] http://www.pwc.com/gx/en/managing-tomorrows-people/future-of-work/pdf/mtp-future-of-work.pdf

[14] http://blog.coldwellbanker.com/homes-for-dogs/

[15]http://make-a-donation.org/articles/what-is-socially-responsible-marketing/

[16]https://www.multinationalmonitor.org/hyper/issues/1991/10/doyle.html

[17]https://www.wsj.com/articles/starbucks-plans-to-cut-plastic-straws-from-stores-globally-by-2020-1531134924

[18]https://www.danone.com/about-danone/sustainable-value-creation/our-vision.html

[19]http://www.un.org/sustainabledevelopment/sustainable-development-goals/

[20]http://www.charlotteobserver.com/news/business/article69251877.html

[21]https://www.christies.com/about-us/corporate-social-responsibility/awards-and-recognitions/

[22]https://blogs.volunteermatch.org/volunteeringiscsr/2013/11/26/the-why-behind-employee-volunteer-time-off/

[23]http://time.com/4965293/kendall-jenner-cries-addresses-pepsi-ad-backlash/

[24]https://www.wired.com/2017/04/pepsi-ad-internet-response/

[25]https://digiday.com/marketing/inside-pepsis-house-content-agency/

[26]http://adage.com/article/cmo-strategy/brad-jakeman-leaving-pepsico-start-a-consultancy/310943/

[27]http://www.adweek.com/agencyspy/heres-the-problem-with-that-content-studio-you-just-built/129188

[28]https://www.nytimes.com/2017/10/08/business/dove-ad-racist.html?_r=0

[29]https://news.nationalgeographic.com/2016/10/wildlife-watch-failed-ivory-trade-CITES-proposals/

[30]http://sustainabilityreport2016.volkswagenag.com/economy/integrity.html

[31]Wall Street Journal, Nov. 17, 2017

[32]https://www.reuters.com/article/us-volkswagen-usa-electric/volkswagen-to-install-2800-u-s-electric-vehicle-charging-stations-idUSKBN1EC1RL

[33]www.bloomberg.com/bcause

[34]https://data.bloomberglp.com/company/sites/28/2017/05/17_0516_Impact-Book_Final.pdf

[35]https://www.sustainablebrands.com/news_and_views/walking_talk/emmanuel_faber/food_human_right_not_commodity

[36]https://www.unglobalcompact.org/take-action/action/value-driver-model#toolkit

[37]https://www.fastcompany.com/40443099/this-pickle-company-achieved-zero-food-waste-by-turning-scraps-into-compost-and-bloody-mary-mix

[38]https://sampi.co/taobao-villages-china-rural-ecommerce/

[39]http://www.ussif.org/content.asp?contentid=71

[40]https://corpgov.law.harvard.edu/2017/07/27/esg-reports-and-ratings-what-they-are-why-they-matter/#1b

[41]http://breakthrough.unglobalcompact.org

[42]http://report.businesscommission.org/report

[43]http://breakthrough.unglobalcompact.org/site/assets/files/1756/guide-breakthrough-pitch_14nov17-1.pdf

[44]https://www.economist.com/business/2012/10/06/call-in-the-b-team

[45]https://www.governanceprinciples.org

[46]https://www.wsj.com/articles/blackrock-companies-should-have-at-least-two-female-directors-1517598407

[47]https://www.wsj.com/articles/new-york-state-fund-snubs-all-male-boards-1521538321

[48]https://www.cnbc.com/2018/05/10/mark-zuckerbergs-control-of-facebook-is-like-a-dictatorship-calstrs.html

[49]https://www.scribd.com/document/325810409/The-Global-Competitiveness-Report-2016-WEF-2017

[50]http://www.chinadevelopmentbrief.cn/news/tencent-launches-chinas-first-internet-philanthropy-day/

[51]https://www.fastcompany.com/40500978/this-new-blockchain-project-gives-homeless-new-yorkers-a-digital-identity

[52]https://www.forbes.com/sites/suparnadutt/2017/09/01/blockchain-is-slowly-changing-digital-banking-in-india-thanks-to-these-startups/#35127844a172

[53]https://www.fool.com/investing/2018/04/11/20-real-world-uses-for-blockchain-technology.aspx

[54]https://www-03.ibm.com/press/us/en/pressrelease/53013.wss